Praise for Florida Landmarks, Lodgings and Legends

Greacen's fond drawings and commentary are nothing less than a rhapsody to many of the Bay Area locations and landmarks that we must remember to appreciate. This collection reminds us.
Tim Dorsey, best-selling Florida novelist

Charley skillfully combines his iconic artistic style with an eye for the humor and history of the featured locations, with delightful results. A treasure for Tampa natives and an invitation to newcomers to learn about "Tampa Town."
James L. Ferman, chairman, Ferman Automotive Management

History sometimes can be fleeting - lost to time - or perhaps even worse, dry and boring. Through his delicate and detailed black and white drawings that resemble etchings, well known Tampa artist Charles Greacen perfectly captures the 120 or so city and state landmarks and other points of interest. He adds color through his research and memories, bringing history to life.
We particularly enjoyed how he portrayed Florida's oldest restaurant, the iconic Columbia in Ybor City.
Richard Gonzmart, 4th generation owner of the Columbia and President of the Columbia Restaurant Group

Charley's attention to detail and personal knowledge of these iconic structures make for a winning combination.
Steve Otto, columnist, The Tampa Tribune

Artist Charles Greacen is a Tampa treasure, as the contents of this extraordinary book clearly reveal. Greacen has brought his unique style to bring to life some of Tampa's most beloved buildings honoring the legacy of the city's fascinating history, its culture and its rich diversity. In addition to capturing the classic architecture of such landmark buildings as The Cuban Club and Union Station, Greacen's often funny, but always pointed recollections of his personal experiences with his subjects leavens this book's appeal for native Tampans and visitors alike. This book is a joy to read and deserves a place in every Tampan's library.
Daniel Ruth, journalist & Pulitzer Prize co-recipient

There are so many worthy but overlooked and under celebrated places in the state of Florida that I am thrilled that Charley Greacen is turning his talents to showing them off. His manner of both drawing and writing is comfortable and intimate. Charley's pen-and-ink drawing capture the spirit and form of these varied places with details that make you appreciate them afresh. His words bring these buildings to life with his anecdotes and observations. I feel like he's driving me around and sharing the back stories of what we're seeing.
As a longtime local preservationist I'm grateful for this book because Charley's drawings and tales will help everyone to fall in love with these places, rich in character, personality and soul.
Linda Saul-Sena, former Tampa City Council member and local preservationist

Charles Greacen's anthology of Tampa Bay landmarks mingles civic pride with a wistful affection for the past. Well-known and long followed for his wry humor, the talented artist and history buff draws upon four decades of illustrating the local arts and cultural scene, complemented with fun facts and personal anecdotes. It's a treasure - and so is Charley.
Amy Scherzer, society chronicler, Tampa Bay Times

Long-time Tampa illustrator and cartoonist Charles Greacen has created a series of iconic images of his adopted city and state. But he hasn't stopped there. Each illustration is accompanied by a short essay that offers history, a bit of whimsy and some of Charley's own memories to create a unique view of these well known places.
Paul Wilborn, author Cigar City, Tales From a 1980's Creative Ghetto

Florida Landmarks, Lodgings & Legends;
Drawings and sometimes accurate accounts
by Charles Greacen

All art and narrative contained in this work is the original work of the author.

Published by St. Petersburg Press
St. Petersburg, FL
www.stpetersburgpress.com

Copyright ©2021

All rights reserved. No part of this publication may be reproduced, distributed, or transmitted in any form or by any means, including photocopying, recording or other electronic or mechanical methods, without the prior written permission of the publisher, except in the case of brief quotations embodied in critical reviews and certain other noncommercial uses permitted by copyright law. For permission requests contact St. Petersburg Press at www.stpetersburgpress.com.

Design and composition by St. Petersburg Press and Isa Crosta
Cover design and artwork by Charles Greacen

Print ISBN: 978-1-940300-50-4
eBook ISBN: 978-1-940300-51-1

First Edition

Florida Landmarks, Lodgings & Legends;
Drawings and sometimes accurate accounts
by Charles Greacen

HYDE PARK 13

1808 Richardson Place 15
1808 Richardson Detail 17
Anderson Park Gates 19
Himes-Griffin House 21
Morrison House 23
Anderson-Frank House 25
810 S. Newport Avenue 27
850 Willow Avenue 29
901 S. Newport Avenue 31
903 S. Delaware Avenue 33
1311 Morrison Avenue 35
1101 Bayshore Boulevard 37
902 S. Delaware Avenue 39
847 S. Newport Avenue 41
917 S. Orleans Avenue 43
Taliaferro House 45
Hutchinson House 47
Peter O. Knight Honeymoon House 49

St. John's Episcopal Church 51
Gorrie Elemantary School 53
Old Hyde Park Art Center 55
Friday Morning Musicale 57
Bern's Steak House 59
Tiny Tap Tavern 61
Spanish-American War Memorial at Plant Park 63
Old Schoolhouse 65
Plant Hall, south porch 67

DOWNTOWN 69

Tampa City Hall 71
Federal Courthouse 73
Tampa Convention Center 75
Amalie Arena 79
Glazer Children's Museum 81
Tampa Museum of Art 83
Tampa Firefighters Museum 85
SS American Victory 87
The Florida Aquarium 89
Tampa Union Station 91
Cruise Terminal 2 93
Sacred Heart Catholic Church 95
Northern Trust 97
Bay View Hotel 99
Tampa Bay History Center 101
Floating Ballpark 103

YBOR CITY 105

Centro Asturiano de Tampa 107
The Cuban Club 109
The German-American Club 111
The Italian Club of Tampa 113
The Casino Theatre 115
Seidenberg Cigar Company 117
Ybor Square 119
The Castle 121
Ybor City Casitas 123
Ferlita Bakery 125
The Columbia Restaurant 127
Las Novedades 129
Cephas Hot Shop 131
El Pasaje 133
The Don Vicente 135
Ybor Victorian house 137

DAVIS ISLANDS 139

Peter O. Knight Airport 141
202 Riviera Avenue 143
The Mirasol Apartments 145
The Palace of Florence 147

ALL ELSE TAMPA 149

IMAX Dome Theatre at MOSI 151
MOSI Recyclosaurus 153
Inkwood Books 155

Jose Gaspar Pirate Ship	157	
405 S. Manhattan Avenue	159	
USF Marshall Student Center	161	
Robinson High School	163	
H.B. Plant High School	165	
Hillsborough High School	167	
Academy of Holy Names	169	
Four Schools	171	
Port Tampa City Library	175	
West Tampa Branch Library	177	
St. James House of Prayer Episcopal Church	179	
3302 W. Mullen Avenue	181	
Jim Cornwell State Farm Insurance	183	
Jimmy Mac's	185	
3215 W. Wallcraft Avenue	187	

Bob Baggett Photography	189
Clawds Crustacean-American Cuisine	191
Streetcar Stations	193
Ballast Point Pier	195
El Centro Espanol of West Tampa	197
Sulphur Springs Water Tower	199
Fort Homer Hesterly Armory	201
Robertson billard table	203

East of Tampa 205

Cracker Country	207
Brandon homestead	209
Sugar cane mill	211
C.C. Smith General Store	213
Enterprise United Methodist Church	215
Annie Pfeiffer Chapel	217

PINELLAS COUNTY 219

Tarpon Springs Area Historical Museum	221
McMullen-Coachman Log Cabin	223
Park Feed Store	225
Perry Snell House	227
Museum of Fine Arts	229
The Florida Holocaust Museum	231
The Dali	233
St. Petersburg Pier	235

SOUTH FLORIDA 237

Sunshine Skyway Bridge	239
Wiggins Store	241
Old Cabbage Head	243
Anna Maria City Pier	245
Anna Maria City Jail	247
Chickee	249
Gamble Mansion	251
Ca' d'Zan at the John and Mable Ringling Museum of Art	253

Edison Winter Home	255
Ford Winter Home	257
Cardozo Hotel	259
Pigeon Key railroad workers' dormitory	261
The Audubon House	263
Ernest Hemingway Home and Museum	265
Key West Lighthouse	267

NORTH FLORIDA 269

Yulee Sugar Mill Ruins State Park	271
Merrily Bed & Breakfast	273
Micanopy Historical Society Museum	275
Historic Haile Homestead	277
Century Tower	279
The Florida State Capitol	281
Fort Matanzas Monument	283
Gonzalez-Alvarez House	285

Acknowledgements

My thanks to the following folks: Herb Hiller's brilliantly written essays in "A Guide to Florida's Small and Historic Lodgings" put my accompanying illustrations in an award-winning book. Audrie Ranon, who managed at least five Tampa Bay-area museum stores, encouraged me to focus my pen-and-ink work on Ybor City's legacy buildings. Fred Hearns, former City of Tampa Community Affairs Director and Curator of Black History at the Tampa Bay History Center, engaged my services to illuminate his self-guided history map with a broad scope of area landmarks.

Kim MacCormack and Mary Scourtes Greacen performed near miracles, using their well-honed, newspaper editing skills to turn my scattered thoughts into plausible reading. Lastly, Amy Cianci paved the way that turned a pile of words and drawings into this book.

Introduction

When asked why I like to draw buildings my simple answer is that buildings don't ever complain that you make them look fat.

The real truth is that buildings do speak to me. No, not in a creepy, haunted-house way or anything like that, but through styles, materials, and proportions, buildings tell much about their creators' hopes and aspirations.

Respect has to be paid to the fact that most of these structures have lifespans far longer than our own. Lifespan is not inappropriate here; buildings are far more organic than they initially appear. Not too dissimilar from the way our own bodies constantly replace cells, our houses, schools, and stores undergo the replacement of roofs, windows, hardware, utilities, and more, throughout their existences. It is not unrealistic to think of these structures as shared exoskeletons that we shape around the ways we live, learn, and work.

When I moved sight-unseen to Florida I discovered a delightfully welcoming population and a rich diversity of architecture. Both continue to make me proud to call this my home.

Charles Greacen

HYDE PARK

Our former home, a Mediterranean-revival house, was built in 1924 right in the middle of Florida's real estate boom. It sits at a quirky zig-zag on Tampa's Richardson Place, evidence that it had been developers and speculators, not urban planners, who laid out city streets. Half a block over runs Bayshore Boulevard, Tampa's prominent waterfront drive. After the boom went bust, the Civilian Conservation Corps would enhance the boulevard with a nearly five-mile-long balustrade and sidewalk.

The Sibleys live there today. This is the first home for their daughter and son. I had the good fortune to be jogging by the house after they arrived from the hospital with both newborns. It was almost a flashback. Many years earlier, Mary Denise and I brought our children, likewise first our daughter and then our son, to this same home. That place is packed with wonderful memories and great vibes.

The fact that I was jogging by wasn't much of a coincidence. Within a week of moving there, I went for a run on Bayshore Boulevard. I'd never been a runner but with the city's best path a half-block away, it was time to try. It worked. I was hooked. When we moved 16 years later we didn't move far and I reconfigured my route to continue to take in my old street. There were too many good neighbors and memories not to return. As that third decade of running was coming to a close, my knees informed me that we had to come to a compromise. We agreed on walking for the next three decades and then to negotiate after that. The first ten years of walking lived up to expectations.

1808 Richardson Place

We found two sets of blueprints when we bought our Richardson Place house. The first was for the small, one-story mudroom that had been added to the house in the 1950's. The second set was for an additional bedroom that would sit on top of the mudroom and jut out past it on the back side. The bedroom had never made it off the drawing board but we saved the blueprints. Years later, after learning the stork was going to make a second visit to our home, we dusted off those plans. On our revised version, to provide the space we wanted, we kept jutting the room out farther and farther until it looked pretty likely to tip over. That is when it occurred to us that our front porch and porte cochere were held up by low-slung arches and they hadn't tipped over, so why not add some to the bedroom? Just before we got underway I took a "before" picture, planning to follow up with an "after" shot. That led to lots of in-progress photos, which eventually led up to a stop-motion documentation of the job. The new bedroom worked out fine but like the old saying, "happily ever after only happens in fairy tales," we would move on to a larger space within three years. Being the devil's advocate, when we handed over the keys I left the two old plans, the plans for our addition and plans for a super-deluxe addition, which I dreamed up just in case we had ever won the lottery.

These should be the gates leading to Kate Jackson Park. Many think they are. Kate Jackson was a successful business person and the driving force behind many Tampa civic improvements. In 1881, she was involved in the creation of the Academy of the Holy Names. Jackson started the Tampa Civic Association in 1911. Adopting the slogan "agitate and educate," she championed street paving and proper drainage. Her greatest point of pride was the development of Tampa's first public playgrounds. Had she been male, she probably could have been Tampa's mayor just like her father, John Jackson. Tampa wasn't ready for that. Kate would have to wait until her 60th year when the passage of the 19th Amendment gave her the right to vote. Tampa wouldn't elect a female mayor until Sandra Freedman took office in 1986, 46 years after Kate Jackson died.

The city of Tampa eventually honored Jackson by naming its Hyde Park recreation center for her. Even this would hold one more slight. Her name ends at the threshold of the building that sits in Anderson Park. Another female, civic activist, Norma Jean Lykes, generously gave her time and money toward building the park's ornate gates and improving its worn-out playground.

Anderson Park Gates

The imposing brick home half a block up my street is known to local historians as the Himes-Griffin House, but our kids Alexandra and Scott call it the Lion King House. It wasn't the granite keystones, slate roof or theatrical balcony that caught their attention, instead they were captivated by the huge lion statues flanking its front steps. The house was built for Tampa city attorney William Fraser Himes, the namesake of Himes Avenue. Construction began in 1909; it would take two years before he and his family moved in. The next owners, Exchange Bank president James A. Griffin and his family, would reside here from 1925 until 1959. In the '40s, the Griffins attached the kitchen, originally a separate structure, to the rest of the house because food had a tendency to get chilly from pot to table. When we moved onto the street, neighborhood children and adults were intrigued by the place as it was uninhabited for several decades. Since then, it has been fully and lovingly refurbished. The main house of the almost 10,000-square-foot mansion features 6 ½ bathrooms, seven bedrooms, eight fireplaces and a huge third-floor ballroom. Its massive lot sits so deep that the back alley was realigned to provide more space, and so wide that it matches four corresponding lots across the street. When Dan O'Connell lived in one of those homes, he claimed the Himes-Griffin was such an attention grabber, he would only see the backs of people's heads walking by.

Himes-Griffin House

If the Morrison House was in Orlando there would be people lined up to tour the haunted house. Since this is the oldest surviving house in Tampa's Hyde Park, perhaps there is a ghost or two under its roof. In 1879, when William Morrison built his house in the middle of his orange groves there were only a few rudimentary farms scattered around the Tampa peninsula. He built his home from concrete blocks made on site. The blocks were formed in specialty molds that gave them the look of ashlar dressed stones. Similar blocks were used to form a retaining wall around his front lawn. A newer house now stands between Morrison's house and the street that bears his name but that wall still runs down to Morrison Avenue as it delineates the original yard. Even though this villa has become landlocked with surrounding homes, its tower still affords panoramic views of the bay and downtown Tampa. More accurately, I should say it once again affords those views. The original cupola and tower were blown away by a hurricane in the '20s. Fifty years later, contractor John Anderson got the commission to restore the home and replace that defining feature. This was his first project after completing a much humbler addition to our home. One of the perks of hiring John was getting to climb up into the unfinished campanile.

Morrison House

Soon after I arrived in Tampa I was invited to a Victorian lawn party on the porch of the Victorian and Queen Anne-style Anderson-Frank House. The event was not as elegant as the name suggests. Two of the attendees were renters who went by the names, Pig and Rat. Although the house never became dilapidated, this represented its lowest ebb. That front porch and the house it's attached to has seen more than its share of change since James Anderson built it in 1901.

I like to picture the home passing through time as in the movie version of H.G. Wells' novel, "The Time Machine." The show starts with a young Tampa still blushing from the attention received from its Spanish-American War support. Bayshore Boulevard was still a muddy path, traversed by horse-drawn buggies. Out in the nearby bay, two swampy islands blossom into self-contained neighborhoods, seemingly in the blink of an eye. More houses and businesses emerge all around Anderson's home. The city's hospital just across the water burgeons, heirs sell the house, and numerous business signs flicker in the front yard. An advertising agency, Marcelina (a private club for women), Fiss Fights (a law firm) and other companies, scoot in and out. Ideally the cinematographer would vignette a collection of Princess Diana's gowns that took up residence here. If the movie is to stop here and not try to predict the future, it will have a happy ending, because the house never looked better.

Anderson-Frank House

This house, which sits a block away from my own, used to belong to a dear friend, Dada Pittman Glaser. She spent many years raising her three children here. I'm happy that downsizing has only taken her a few blocks over because she is one of those people who makes your day a little better any time you encounter her. Some credit for this has to go to her dad whom I met long before I met Dada. Shortly after I moved to Tampa I got a job at The Tampa Tribune & The Tampa Times. One day as I was entering the elevator I was joined by an older, unassuming fellow. He extended a hand and drawled, "Hi, How'r yew, I'm Red Pitman." I shook his hand and introduced myself. He then asked where I worked. I replied, "They've got me in customer services; where do they have you?" Red smiled, benignly, and said, "Oh, they have me bein' publisher."

There weren't enough shades of red to express my embarrassment. He just followed up with, "Nice to meet you, Charley," as he got off at his stop. This remarkable gentleman truly made it his business to try to know every employee at our newspaper. No clerk, pressman or janitor, was unimportant in his thinking. Four years later, when I made a career move, he called me to his office to ask where I was going and what were my thoughts on my experience at the paper.

How I wish there were more executives like him.

810 S. Newport Avenue

When the English brought the bungalow concept home from India they got something more exotic than functional. Eventually, these homes would be transplanted onto more fertile ground. In Australia, coastal California, and along the Gulf of Mexico, conditions were far better suited for the virtues of the bungalow. At the outset of the 20th Century, America had developed a taste for the arts and crafts aesthetic movement, which married perfectly with the bungalow's architectural elements. The exposed rafters and decorative brackets contributed a homespun feel to these unpretentious homes. The ability to mitigate heat in a pre-air conditioned age was another big part of their appeal. Porches and broad roof overhangs offered shade and allowed windows to remain open during a rainstorm. Casement windows effectively scooped breezes into the homes. Bungalows turned out to be as functional in Tampa as they were in Bengali, where they originated. This particular example, the home of Michael and Laurie Kipphut, is as close to a textbook example as you will find. The only drawback I've heard is owners of bungalows with porte cocheres find these coverings were engineered more for Model Ts than Chevy Suburbans.

850 Willow Avenue

Tampa historians call this the Henderson house because Greenville Henderson built it for his family in 1910. I refer to it as the Sykes house since they are the only owners I've known and the Sykes' have been here longer than the Hendersons. They are the only owners that ever gave my son and me Tampa Bay Rays baseball tickets. The Sykes are civic boosters and engaging neighbors. When our community was awarded an MLB expansion franchise, John Sykes and the company he created, Sykes Enterprises, supported the program. Their sponsorship provided them with an abundance of tickets, so they shared them with employees, civic groups and "Basketball Boy."

Basketball Boy was the little kid that dribbled a ball past their house, going to and from school twice a day. Susan Sykes was one of a number of neighbors who marked the time by the sound of his dribble. One neighbor lamented she sometimes overslept when school was out and the familiar bouncing sound didn't wake her. "Basketball Boy" was our son Scott. When he got his first taste of basketball at the YMCA, he was smitten. I mentioned that his uncle, my brother Bob, used his walks to school to develop his ball-handling skills. Those skills eventually earned Bob Greacen an NBA championship ring (he was a second-round draft pick for the Milwaukee Bucks). Scott began dribbling the next morning. He got to be pretty good with basketball, too. Not NBA-good, but good enough to score us some Rays tickets, five-rows up and right behind home plate.

901 S. Newport Avenue

When you have lived in a home for a quarter of a century it is likely you've seen a lot of people come and go. Although we don't have the longevity record for our block, we have seen much turnover. The Corcells' home, a block away, has had four owners while we've been here. This drawing was done when Ted and Judy Waller were our friendly neighbors. They were fun. Judy had a fetish for trying out new businesses. I remember her apiary - yes, she became a bee farmer. Another time, she opened an antique shop. If I were one of those opportunistic types, I would have tried to sell her logos for all her enterprises. Come to think of it, I did.

One year, during our city's annual Gasparilla pirate parade, they hosted a fun party featuring entertainment by Otis Day. He reprised his Otis Day & The Knights role from the 1978 movie "Animal House." The guy still had it. One of those keepsake family memories is dancing ecstatically to "Shout" with my wife and daughter one evening. I already had earned my creds with his band. Otis had begun the "do-da-loo-do" keyboard lead-in to the R&B classic "Any Day Now" and introduced it as a Curtis Mayfield song. I shook my head "no" and stage-whispered, "Chuck Jackson." There is no convincing me that those guys didn't work just a bit harder knowing there was another blues hound in the room.

903 S. Delaware Avenue

I drew this for Sally and Brad Welch and their three sons when they lived here. Their home was built early in the last century and originally looked out at orange groves and Hillsborough Bay. Brad, my former stockbroker, enjoyed coaching baseball teams at our neighborhood Little League fields. The fact is, I've never heard of anyone who doesn't treasure their Little League memories. I was lucky to get to watch both of my children play on teams there. The little waterside complex features a panoramic view of downtown Tampa and the port. It is the only ballpark I've known where games have been halted on account of manatee sightings. Even the kids who didn't play baseball flocked there. Tate Brothers Pizza was around the corner and it was the site of countless celebrations. Even a defeat lost its sting after a pepperoni slice or two. In 2012, I had an experience that underscored how far Bayshore Little League is embedded in the community. I was walking in a crosswalk approaching the Anderson Park gates when a clueless motorist turned and knocked me to the pavement, breaking my hip. Brad and two other Bayshore Little League friends (each from different seasons and different teams) were among the first to rush to my aid. Brad and I didn't always see eye to eye regarding investment advice and I could never figure out how he put together his team's batting orders, but he, and the others, were MVP's that day.

1311 Morrison Avenue

Sherry West hired me to draw her picturesque, Bayshore Boulevard house. The rendering commemorates its recent addition on the left. Adding onto houses in our neighborhood is not a cut-and-dried process. Plans have to be submitted and approved by two separate entities. Since we are part of a historic district any additions go first before the Architectural Review Commission, and after that hurdle is cleared, the city's zoning board. The process can be lengthy and frustrating but it has prevented some ugly, inappropriate modifications from being inflicted on some stately, old homes.

There is a memorable photo of this house taken after the hurricane of 1921, the last storm to deliver a direct hit to the Tampa Bay area. The house looks out at Hillsborough Bay, and in that photo the front had been peeled away by storm surge. A couple of years ago when Hurricane Irma had veered to the west and appeared to be heading our way, I saw Curt Genders, the current owner, who is the king of positive attitude.

"So, what if it hits?," I asked.

He just smiled and said, "I've got tons of insurance and three buildable lots."

1101 Bayshore Boulevard

Hyde Park is a delightful medley of architectural styles. Most of the homes in this neighborhood were built in the first quarter of the 20th Century and they reflect the prevailing trends of that period, bungalow, Mediterranean revival, colonial revival and Florida craftsman were the most popular looks and they turn up nearly on every block. They are all well suited for Tampa's subtropical climate, too. When you are a fan of architecture it can be the exception that ices the cake.

A good example is the Leo Weiss house, at the end of my street, now owned by friends Janelle and Dan Wolff. It is one of only a couple of Tudor-revival residences here. Built in 1929, this ensemble of brick, half-timber and diamond mullions has all the earmarks of a proper, English manor house. Although I have kiddingly given it the pet name Toad Hall by the Bay, I have always admired its aristocratic look. The steep pitch of the roof has to be a plus since leaves can't accumulate there. Also, roof repairs, a topic I've taken on with only qualified success, are clearly something left to the pros. And no neighborhood child has complained about a stranded Frisbee.

902 S. Delaware Avenue

The first time I saw Hyde Park I knew I wanted to live here. After getting to know the neighbors, I knew I'd never leave. With rare exceptions, the families who have chosen to spend their lives here take full advantage of walking the sidewalks and gathering on their porches. Every house has a story or two. This gracious Italian Renaissance domicile has more than its share of tales. Until recently, author Michael Connelly resided here, along with his family. The Philadelphia-born writer and his wife Linda split their time between Hollywood, CA, and Tampa. Some of his best-selling stories (with more than 35 novels that have sold more than 70 million copies) feature LAPD Detective Hieronymus "Harry" Bosch or Los Angeles-based defense attorney Mickey Haller. His novels are instantly recognized by any fan of crime fiction. The novel "The Lincoln Lawyer" was made into a movie starring Matthew McConaughey.

Another former owner, Dr. Joel Mattison, brought his own intriguing stories to the house. After graduation from Davidson University, Mattison studied at Princeton Theological Seminary. Ordained as a Presbyterian minister, Mattison soon realized God had different plans for him so he enrolled in Duke University College of Medicine. He spent his internship with Albert Schweitzer in French Equatorial Africa, which became Gabon. The term "polymath," a person of wide-ranging knowledge or learning, was made for Mattison. His fields of expertise included medicine, law, photography, calligraphy, nature studies and American antiques. In addition, he and his wife Jean always found time to be contributing members of our neighborhood. The new owner has big shoes to fill.

847 S. Newport Avenue

I drew this home when friends Joe and Laraine O'Neill lived here. Joe is a syndicated writer whose column, Opinions to Go, encompasses politics, media issues and sports. I felt I knew the house better than the O'Neills, but it looked very different when Mary Denise and I examined it on our great house hunt of the '90s.

When your wife casually says to you, "I've been thinking about a bigger house," you might as well start packing because you are going to move. One issue was our wish list. Both of us had certain amenities we wanted for a new place. The trouble was that as we saw more real estate we discovered more things we couldn't live without. At the outset of this venture we balanced the virtues of moving versus adding on to our place. In a perverse form of compromise we bought another house and then added onto it. In the course of home hunting we toured what seemed to be every third house in our Hyde Park neighborhood. One of the prospects was the bungalow that would eventually belong to the O'Neills. At that time it had the look of the home of a recluse who had been spending all his time living in a small, neglected room. It was not a good look.

At about the same time we found and committed (a word with multiple, appropriate meanings here) to our "new" 1941 home, the recluse home found a buyer, too. That homeowner had expansion plans that were surprisingly similar to ours. We got to know each other as we wound our way through the city's permitting maze. Once work commenced at our new place I routinely checked it each morning. I also made random spot inspections during my daily jog. Once a week, I'd also take a peek at my new acquaintance's project and the similarities were striking. When Joe and Laraine bought the house I could have walked through it blindfolded.

A quarter of a century has passed since those respective remodelings took place. Joe and Laraine recently moved to a nearby townhouse. The new owners have begun a renovation that substantially expands the building's footprint. Back at our home, I'm simply struggling to keep up with repairs on everything that has worn out in the last 25 years.

917 S. Orleans Avenue

Thomas C Taliaferro is the example of the American dream, having worked his way from teller to president of the First National Bank of Tampa. Of course it didn't hurt that his father was one of the owners of the bank. Clearly, it was a career based on more than nepotism; he would serve as president for 24 years and continue as chairman of the board for another 23 years. His Hyde Park colonial-style house was built in 1890. In 1977, the Women's Survival Center, now named the Helen Gordon Davis Centre for Women, settled into the old Taliaferro House. It continues to be a good fit after more than four decades, offering services to "encourage, elevate and empower women."

One item on T.C. Taliaferro's resume seems more impressive than being a hotshot banker. He was Tampa fire chief for two terms. The fire department in the town where I grew up and the one where I attended college were served by volunteer firefighters. Friends of mine signed on in both towns. I also have friends here who are paid first responders. Far from embracing each other, the pros and the volunteers question each others' motives. Volunteers look on the paid firefighters as mercenaries and the latter view the former as thrill seekers. It can get pretty rancorous. Taliaferro's first task as chief was to merge Tampa's first two fire companies, one paid and one volunteer. Somehow, he pulled off this potentially combustible task.

Taliaferro House

When drugstore owner Currie Hutchinson decided to build a house in his adopted city, he wanted it to look different from his neighbors. When the building was completed in 1908 Hutchinson was the owner of the only Second Empire-style home in the Tampa Bay area. The salient feature of this style is the slate-clad mansard roof. A lack of naturally occurring slate in Florida may help account for the style's rarity here. Also, mansard roofs don't serve their owners as a floor tax dodge as they did back in Second Empire-era France. Hutchinson adopted another feature; this is one of the rare houses in the area to include a basement. This sturdy building was commodious enough to be converted into a hospital. It performed this service between 1931 and 1946. The low ebb came in 1958 when it became the chapter house for a University of Tampa fraternity. Squint and you'll be able to picture the boys of "Animal House" carrying on from the balcony. In 1977, when the university temporarily banned fraternities, the Hutchinson House began its slow march back to respectability.

Attorney Matt Powell, who had rented space in the house since the '80s, bought it in 1999 and continues restoration work. It looks much like it did in the early days, including such touches as the original curb stone, ready to aid arrivals to dismount from their horses.

Hutchinson House

It is ironic that nothing remains from Peter O. Knight's Bayshore mansion he built at the height of his career. We have inherited cottage he and his bride Lillie occupied when he moved to Tampa. Knight arrived at the age of 25 after he had served as the mayor of Fort Myers; his talents were quickly noticed. Between 1893 to 1899, he served as Florida State Attorney, while his day job was as president of Tampa Electric Company from 1924 to 1946. Along the way, he helped create the Exchange Bank of Florida and provided the land for his namesake airport.

His picturesque cottage, now a cherished landmark, huddles in the shadow of the LeRoy Selmon Crosstown Expressway. In the expressway's toll road path, the cottage narrowly escaped being swept away like so many other noteworthy buildings. Witnessing the condemnation process for the road's path was painful. A pair of Victorian houses with matching round turrets, which had been built by a banker as wedding presents for his twin daughters, were demolished soon after I discovered them. A nearby, delightfully eccentric home, made from bricks, stones and whatever the owner could find, joined their fate. The Crosstown permanently chopped in half the tight-knit neighborhood of Dobyville, home to a bustling African-American community that hugs the fringe of Hyde Park. Sorry, but thoughts of that expressway bring out my glass half-empty side.

Peter O. Knight Honeymoon House

My parish, St. John's Episcopal Church, is a short walk from home. The first church was a wooden sanctuary on the site in 1912. This brick building replaced it in 1926. The church inaugurated St. John's Parish Day School in 1951 on the property next door. The school has earned high marks as a learning institution but with success there have been growing pains. Set in an established neighborhood, the school works hard to keep its traffic flow from being an imposition to those residing around it. For the most part, the church and school have been successful.

Another Tampa institution has grown and causes chafing in the neighborhood. The city's annual Gasparilla Pirate Invasion and Parade, an event with more than a whiff of debauchery from marchers and spectators, has always followed a route that hugs Hyde Park. The crowd of onlookers has grown year after year. Through no fault of St. John's or the neighborhood during this local holiday this stretch of the parade became ground zero for teenage drinking. A sad pattern of litter, torn-up landscaping and arrests, marred the area. Things came to a head when teenagers broke into and vandalized St. Johns in 1997.

The church's response was truly inspired. The following year, Leland Baldwin, St. John's youth program director, recruited students and young parishioners to set up a safe house on the premises to administer first aid to any and all who were overindulged. Not only did it head off serious alcohol consequences for many high school-aged partiers and calm behavior in the neighborhood, young volunteers got a sobering lesson about the risks of drinking.

St. John's Episcopal Church

When Gorrie Elementary School opened in 1889 it met criticism for being "out in the boondocks," even though it was only a mile from downtown Tampa. Obviously, its placement wasn't so misguided as it is the oldest elementary school in all of Florida. A less often noted distinction is having the first indoor toilets of any Hillsborough County school. After soon outgrowing the original building, Gorrie's current home was completed in 1903. In 1915, the Hyde Park Grammar School took on the Gorrie name to honor Florida native John Gorrie, the father of refrigeration and air conditioning. Gorrie Elementary School has a student body of approximately 575 attending classes from kindergarten through fifth grade. The "boonies" that Gorrie brushed up against rapidly gave way to the development of fashionable neighborhoods. In stages, the city boundary expanded until it encompassed the entire South Tampa peninsula.

When Mary Denise, a proud Tampa native, was growing up in Palma Ceia she enjoyed all the urban refinements the city had to offer, but by a quirk of geography her family lived in a home just outside the city limits for her first six months. Before she was a year old the city had expanded and taken in her neighborhood. Since then, my wife has lived her whole life in the city she loves.

On rare occasions when I conclude we are suffering from an excess of domestic tranquility, I ask if my little country gal wants to watch some "Hee-Haw" reruns with me. Yes, call me a glutton for punishment.

Gorrie Elemantary School

It seems as though I had just finished drawing the Tampa Realistic Artists' Art Center when the group decided to rebuild the front porch to recreate its earlier look. I briefly considered revising my drawing to match the restoration but quickly dismissed the idea. When a structure gets moved, remodeled and repurposed as often as this little place, any snapshot works. Starting in 1899, this was the temporary home of Gorrie Elementary while the current schoolhouse was built. It was converted into a lunchroom in 1914. Gorrie students could get a hot lunch for a nickel. After a little more remodeling and a nudge over to Swann Avenue, it took on the role of Gorrie's library between 1922 and 1968. A year later it was leased (and finally purchased) by the Tampa Realistic Artists, Inc. and rechristened the Old Hyde Park Art Center. Of course, the building got another round of remodeling during the transition. The Center continues to be an active component of the South Tampa arts community. In case I haven't made it abundantly clear, I'm always in favor of putting old buildings to new uses and creating studio space in particular.

When I studied at Denison University my favorite work space was in Doane Hall, which was built half a century earlier as a gymnasium but now was serving as space for studio arts and art history lectures. It took me a while to realize walls had been put up to divide what had once been a basketball court. That explained why the floor looked like a work by the Dutch painter Piet Mondrian. Workers at some point pulled up the wood flooring and when the boards were relaid, the installers paid no regard to the painted lines, creating a wonderful random series of dots and dashes. I wonder how many artists that floor inspired.

Old Hyde Park Art Center

The Friday Morning Musicale was my mother-in-law's Carnegie Hall. When 97-year-old Christine Scourtes was a little girl, Tampa had numerous movie houses and theaters, but the Musicale was the only conservatory for classical music. Even though it only had seating for 835 people, performing a recital on a Steinway grand piano was a heady experience for the 5-year-old daughter of Greek immigrants. Early in the 20th Century, six local women's clubs banded together to create an incubator for serious musical talents. Hyde Park's Friday Morning Musicale, built in 1927, was the culmination of those efforts. It is a great credit to this organization, and the opportunity for a bad pun by me, to note the Musicale was instrumental in the formation of the Florida Orchestra. Situated in a world that seems to reinvent itself daily, the Musicale remains remarkably unchanged. The stage, the lobby, and even its two, original Steinways, support that original mission. It is thanks to the ongoing efforts that Christine would have the experience of watching her 5-year-old granddaughter, Alexandra, perform her dance recital on that same stage. Alexandra had her own way to make events especially memorable. After the dancers had lined up for their final bows and the curtains had closed, she emerged to make her own personal curtain call. I was mildly mortified, but looking back it was probably a good thing because that turned out to be the pinnacle of her dance career.

Friday Morning Musicale

When I resigned from my first job in New Jersey and told my boss I was moving to Tampa he told me there was a restaurant I must visit: Bern's Steak House. That was nearly 50 years ago but the advice is just as valid today. Bern and Gert Laxer opened the restaurant in 1956 and grew it from a 40-seat cafe to its present 350-guest capacity. Legend has it that Bern's name was selected because it used letters leftover from the property's previous tenant's sign. Along the way, the Laxers earned a reputation for serving the best steaks in town, raising their own organic vegetables and compiling the most comprehensive wine list in the world. There are enough details and praise elsewhere for Bern's that I'll leave that responsibility to others. I'll simply note that Bern's has done things that would be the ruination of lesser restaurants. This institution has spun off a stylish restaurant, Haven; Epicurean, a boutique hotel; and cooking school, Epicurean Theatre. Remarkably neither have been enough of a distraction to make Bern's miss a beat.

One look at my stock portfolio proves I'm not good at predicting things but I feel safe in my prognostication that Bern's will outlive us all. It survived well for its founders and is now capably run by their son, David. Many servers who made Bern's their career have passed. My friend Phil, who created photo murals of Bern's European vineyard trips, has departed. So has Don, a printer, who used to keep the encyclopedic wine list current. At times, when I consider my own mortality and what lies beyond, I'm comforted with the hope that Bern and Gert have set up shop in the great hereafter.

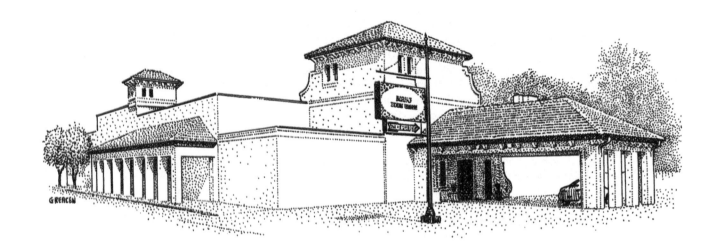

Bern's Steak House

When I moved to Florida, sight unseen, I had the good fortune to wind up in Hyde Park, a neighborhood I've only briefly left. Soon after I arrived I came across a grubby, concrete-block tap room that didn't bother to close its doors. It was love at first sip. Tiny Tap loyalists claim the bar dates back to 1934, but others, who should know, say that back then it was a gas station and it didn't become a bar until 1957. I've considered the possibility it was a gas station that served beer, considering the peculiar drink ways I encountered in this state. (Before I moved here I didn't know there were drive-through liquor stores, like the one I found on Highway 60, which would give you a plastic cup of ice with your pint of whiskey.) The Tap has achieved dive-bar, cult status, which of course is brilliant. When you are a dive bar, bad reviews don't just bounce off you, they burnish your image. If consistency is a virtue, the Tiny Tap is almost holy ground; an upgraded juke box is the only change in the last 45 years I can recall. It's hard to pick a favorite recollection from the bar but this will have to do.

Our porch party at my nearby apartment was running dangerously low on beer so someone suggested we move it to The Tap. Conveniently, I was able to fit everyone onto my flatbed Model A truck to deliver us to The Tap's front door. It was a slow night and we practically had the place to ourselves. Our friend Paul Wilborn commandeered the bar's battered upright piano with mostly working keys and brought the place alive. One of the bar's regulars, a guy who looked as if he would gladly follow Charles Manson, came over and told me he "dug our family." A couple from our group, who took him up on an invitation to his apartment atop then-Hugo's eatery on the next block, reported the evening got a lot weirder. One word of warning, before you put your money in the jukebox make sure there isn't a CSX 97-car train approaching on the tracks next door.

Tiny Tap Tavern

The eyes of the world were on Tampa as our armed forces gathered for the invasion of Cuba at the outbreak of the Spanish-American War. While troops pitched tents in dusty, mosquito-ridden fields in and around the city, officers gave interviews and posed for photographs on the posh porch of the Tampa Bay Hotel, now the University of Tampa.

Veterans erected a memorial in 1927 to that "splendid, little war" crowned with a cannon from that period. That cannon, which had come from a fort that had guarded the mouth of Tampa Bay, was melted down to produce new weapons during World War II. Later, it was replaced with a similar weapon that came from Mobile Bay. The memorial appropriately is situated in Plant Park on the former grounds of that hotel where generals and journalists made news.

If you are an artillery fan there are two pieces of ordinance nearby with a more compelling story. Before the Civil War the government placed three, smoothbore, 24-pounder cannons across the river at Fort Brooke to protect it from attacks. When war came these older guns didn't have the range to prevent federal gunboats from bombarding the fort and town but they could prevent a direct assault. The southern forces were so strapped for provisions the Fort Brooke defenders were drawn away to gather cattle to send to famished troops in adjacent states. In their absence, a small raiding party rowed ashore and disabled the cannons by knocking off their trunnions, the pivots that hold them on their carriages. After the war the useless weapons sat abandoned on the bay's shore until Henry Plant brought two of them to be novel ornaments on the lawn of his Tampa Bay Hotel.

Spanish-American War Memorial at Plant Park

The Old Schoolhouse is shamelessly cute and that probably goes a long way to explain this little scrapper's survival. Gen. Jesse Carter and his family were among the few settlers living on the west side of the Hillsborough River facing Fort Brooke and the little camp follower village that became Tampa. With no bridge to cross the river in 1855 there were limited school options for Carter's children so the resourceful general built one.

Portability also worked in favor of the diminutive building. When Henry Plant bought the land where the school stood to build his sprawling hotel, he assigned the little building such tasks as an apothecary and a tool shed. When needed, the school was scooted across the hotel grounds. The DeSoto Chapter of the Daughters of the American Revolution took this antebellum gem under its wing and initiated restoration in 1931, including an addition at the back of the building. Easily overlooked in the shadows of Plant's pseudo-Moorish extravaganza, the diminutive Old Schoolhouse bears witness to Tampa's wilderness days.

Old Schoolhouse

Long before Walt Disney built his Magic Kingdom's castle in Orlando, Henry B. Plant conjured up a mighty pleasure palace on the bank of Tampa's Hillsborough River. His competitor Henry Flagler also built extravagant hotels along Florida's other coast. Plant used onion-domed minarets to set his resort a world apart. Although the Tampa Bay Hotel was outrageously impractical, the city of Tampa recognized its landmark value and bought it from the Plant family. When the hotel closed in 1932 a barely 2-year-old Tampa Junior College leased the building. This profitable coupling gave birth to today's University of Tampa.

As they approached its first 100 years UT's signature minarets were looking a bit dog-eared. Their symbolism was understood and funds were raised to not just restore but to upgrade the distinctive spires. The old rusted, sheet-metal skins were replaced with dazzling stainless steel.

A few years ago I took my mother-in-law, Christine Scourtes, to her 70th reunion. After getting her degree there she also worked for the university's president and later taught psychology at the university. I had the good fortune to climb to the very top of one of those minarets. I was glad Christine stayed behind. (A former judge lived in a minaret as a student in the '50s in exchange for painting and putting window panes in his little space.) The access is pretty primitive, but the view is well worth it.

Wonder how many water balloons have been thrown from this strategic perch?

Plant Hall, south porch

DOWNTOWN

The city of Tampa built its first city hall in 1890. The mayor, city council, city clerk's office, along with the police and the fire departments, were squeezed into the stubby, two-story brick building. City fathers called for a much-needed do over 25 years later and this time they got it right. Tampa's architectural teacher's pet, M. Leo Elliot, designed a nine-story beaux arts-layer cake that still works and looks good more than a century after it was completed. There was no allowance for a clock in the budget until a fundraising campaign by a precocious teen Hortense Oppenheimer shamed civic leaders into paying for one. The timepiece has been known as Hortense ever since.

Tampa owes its existence to Fort Brooke, a military camp dedicated to snuffing out the Seminole Indian presence in Central Florida. Possibly unaware of the irony, Elliot placed the dispassionate visages of four Seminole maidens on each side, just under the building's cornice.

City council and the city clerk's office periodically buy my coffee mugs with this image fired onto them. Three years ago, a delegation from City Hall took a batch to Cuba to hand out as goodwill gifts. I could almost hear the cries of "Viva las Tejas Ciudades" (roughly, hurray for Town Tiles) from here.

Tampa City Hall

The old Federal Courthouse in downtown Tampa looks thoroughly grand but all three of its original occupants eventually would outgrow it. That air of grandeur was the work of James Knox Taylor, supervising architect for the U.S. Treasury. In 1905, it was shared by the U.S. Post Office, U.S. Customs and the U.S. District Court. When the last of the three moved to more adequate quarters, the building stood empty for 15 years. In 2014, after 16 months of much-needed renovation, repairs and upgrades, the old building became the home of Le Meridien, a 130-room, boutique hotel and Bizou Brasserie restaurant. The grand exterior and exceptional architecture is matched with a plush lobby while its concierge desk is an old judge's desk.

The Federal Court moved a few blocks uptown to the Sam Gibbons Courthouse. Gibbons, a South Tampa native was honored for his heroic record during World War II and the 17 terms he served in the U.S. House of Representatives. Sam Gibbons, for all his accolades and access to power, was as down to earth a man as you could hope to meet. Many years ago, Mary Denise and I happened across a yard sale the Gibbons' were holding where we purchased a bench for our front porch. (Even war heroes hold yard sales.) Of course, we dubbed this our congressional seat. To our disappointment, despite glue and repeated clamping, the bench did not prove as enduring as Sam's career in Washington.

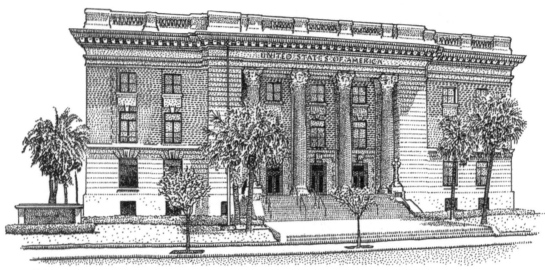

Federal Courthouse

When Tampa Convention Center opened in 1990 all it had to do to meet public expectations was to look less like the grille of a Ford Edsel, as its predecessor did. The new center actually went far beyond the old Curtis Hixon Convention Hall in size, style, and location. Curtis Hixon sat tantalizingly close to the Hillsborough River, downtown, but it had the Tampa Museum of Art's former building squeezed between it and any water views. The new center, at the mouth of that river, enjoys a sweeping view of two islands and the Bay beyond. That guarantees convention goers from Fort Wayne, IN, don't soon forget their Tampa experience. As for size, the 600,000-square-foot facility could swallow whole its 62,000 square-foot predecessor. The functional, cantilevered levels of the new building are so unassuming you hardly are aware the building actually straddles traffic coming across the bridge from Bayshore Boulevard.

I used to jog around the convention center daily before my weary knees overruled the route. The variety of gatherings advertised on the marquee is mind-boggling and entices me. For example, when the convention center hosts Tampa Bay Comic Con, that whole corner of downtown becomes a phantasmagoria of costumed-characters living out their wildest dreams. I go there, walk home, look myself in the mirror, and all nagging feelings of self doubt melt away.

Tampa Convention Center

Along with the former Tampa Bay Hotel, Tampa Theatre comes in among our city's finest, historic architectural treasures. Built in 1926, the theater's lavish interior was as much of the show as any movie on the screen. After passing through its ornate lobby, theatergoers enter a baroque, rococo Spanish courtyard, dressed up with statuary and colonnades. As the house lights dim, twinkling stars and floating clouds enliven its simulated sky overhead. Better still, before every show the theatre's mighty Wurlitzer organ rises from below the stage to serenade an audience. The movie house also was Tampa's first commercial building to offer the novel comfort of air conditioning. In 1973, the theater almost succumbed to the wrecking ball. It is now supported by loyal members and concert attendance. Major digital upgrades make it possible to schedule an extensive offering of first run and classic films. Among the long and diverse list of acts who performed on the stage, I've enjoyed Randy Newman, B.B. King, The Police and Harry Chapin. It was a privilege to perform one of my favorite weddings on Tampa Theatre's stage. In the lights on the marquee was a message that probably sums up every good marriage: "Tina Lorino and Jimmy Rice - You've Met Your Match."

Tampa Theatre

When I heard about the notion to bring a National Hockey League expansion team to Tampa the expression "snowball's chance in hell" seemed appropriate. Tampa kids play baseball, basketball, football (both kinds), tennis, and golf, all year long. Their exposure to hockey up to then was pretty limited. Hockey, are you kidding me? Was I wrong. When the Lightning struck Tampa Bay, it struck gold. Sellout crowds convinced the city that the team needed an arena and Tampa had the Ice Palace up and running for the team's second season. When the Lightning first brought the Lord Stanley Cup home the team shared it with enraptured fans all year long.

In 2002, the year I started selling my weekly cartoon to the St. Petersburg Times, now the Tampa Bay Times, the paper bought the arena's naming rights. Naming the downtown Tampa sports venue the St. Petersburg Times Forum was a circulation war, slap-in-the-face to hometown paper, The Tampa Tribune. This war was fatal for The Tribune and a Pyrrhic victory for the Times.

In 2014, the local Amalie Oil Company renamed the stadium the Amalie Arena, and uses it for ice hockey, basketball and concerts. The financially strapped Times needed the naming money (at least I'll go to the grave claiming so) to pay to run my cartoons.

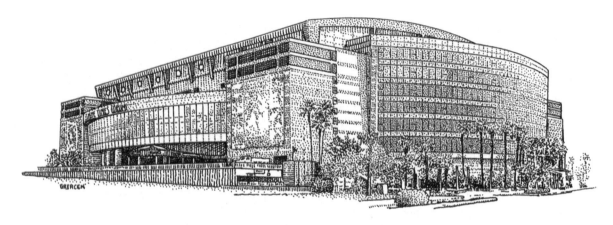

Amalie Arena

Glazer Children's Museum has a policy that adult visitors must be accompanied by a child. Unfortunately, I'm at an age where I need my children to find a child so I can qualify for admission. The imaginative looking museum in Tampa houses 170 interactive exhibits within its 53,000 square-foot interior. Most of those exhibits serve the laudable goal of teaching through playing. This giant toy box opened in 2010 in the Waterfront Arts District next to the Tampa Museum of Art. Its roots go back a quarter of a century to more humble beginnings.

In 1986, the Tampa Children's Museum occupied retail space in the less-than-prestigious Floriland Mall. In 1989, the museum found a far better fit when it leased Safety Village at Lowry Park in Seminole Heights. Built in 1965, Safety Village was a miniaturized version of downtown Tampa where children could learn traffic rules and to not spit on the sidewalk. When the Children's Museum moved downtown, Tampa bulldozers moved in and the village, along with neighboring Fairyland, were gone forever. Gone also was the adjacent, quaint amusement park where my wife still accuses me of putting our daughter on the "ride of death."

The park's dinky roller coaster reduced Alexandra and her sidekick, Jenny, to tears. I had to plead with the operator to abruptly stop to let them off after the first go-around. That brought me a lot of heat at home. The tension escalated a week later when one of the ride's little cars snapped free flying off its tracks with two people aboard. It seemed that local stations re-ran that story for three weeks; the lectures never let up.

Glazer Children's Museum

Architect Stanley Saitowitz endowed the Tampa Museum of Art's building with a split personality. By day, it strikes the eye as a monolithic fortress. Its pierced aluminum skin forcefully avoids any interplay with the changing daylight sky. At night, its other personality comes out to play. The LED lighting Saitowitz knit into the exterior turns the museum into a kaleidoscopic glowworm intent on soothing the eye and spirit. TMA borders Old Tampa's waterfront Curtis Hixon Park and the welcoming shade cast by its cantilevered galleries lures visitors into the lobby like a passive pitcher plant.

As a relatively newer museum, TMA has made scheduling quality traveling exhibits its priority. Its large, simplistic gallery space lends itself well for this mission. The museum's exception to this model is the incomparable collection of Greco-Roman art and artifacts on permanent display. In 1986, Joseph Veach Noble bequeathed some 150 pieces of classical art he had gathered during his lifetime. The museum has continued building this collection and it now numbers more than 600 items. Probably not everyone gets as excited as I do over Athenian red-figured pottery or Roman coin portraiture, but I have to make an effort not to drool each time I enter this part of the museum.

Among my possessions I have a few bits of ceramics and whatnots from Europe. When we traveled in England, Mary Denise noticed I always picked towns that ended in Caster or Chester to spend the night. That's because it indicated a fortified Roman town or castra once stood there with ancient artifacts just waiting to be discovered. It's hard to even look at my paltry stuff after a visit to TMA.

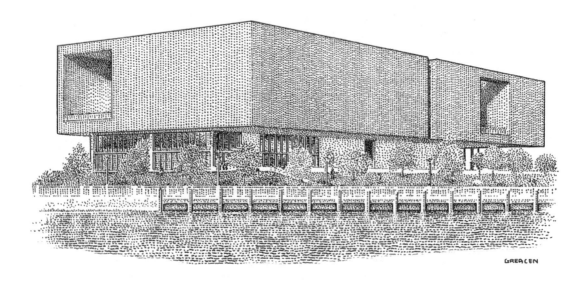

Tampa Museum of Art

Tampa's fire department was a mere 27 years away from its bucket brigade days when its headquarters was built in 1911. Between that year and 1978, when it was replaced, the building would witness the evolution of firefighting from the era of horse-drawn vehicles and curbside-call boxes to diesel-powered pumpers and wireless communication. Tampa Firefighters Museum has an extensive collection of equipment documenting this story. Adding continuity, the new facility is just across the street.

Tampa is dotted with a number of historic firehouses that have outlived their original purpose. Sadly, there is a marker where Station #4 stood, explaining it was going to be a museum but was lost to a "bureaucratic blunder." Metal sculptor Dominique Martinez bought old #5 in Seminole Heights and has turned it into a home and studio. It is a showplace figuratively and literally. Two 1920s-era, deconsecrated firehouses remain in Hyde Park. Old Station #8 home to a trailer park management company, has had much of its charm glossed over, but old #3 at Platt Street and Magnolia Avenue, still looks ready to respond to all calls, even though it is a private home. One of our neighborhood carpenters gave me a tour while it was undergoing its transformation. Two favorite features are the circular glass, brick shower stall that protrudes into the living space and the floor hatches that allow one to use the fire poles if in a hurry to depart.

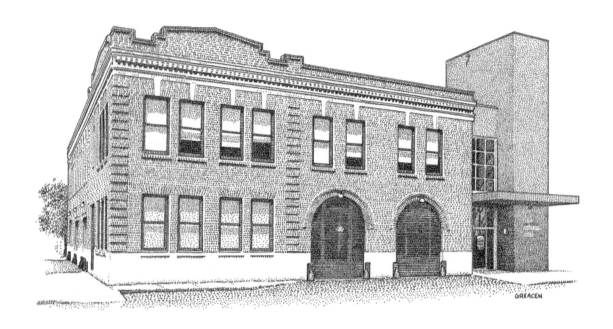

Tampa Firefighters Museum

Hopefully the SS American Victory is here to stay. The 85-year-old liberty ship is one of only four afloat today from the 2,710 launched during World War II. After serving the military during WWII, the Korean Conflict and Vietnam, the ship made its way to Tampa in 1999. American Victory is moored adjacent to the Florida Aquarium and is open for tours daily.

The "hopefully" part comes from the fact that another nautical relic came and went. Just like the Victory, the submarine USS Requin was launched just as WWII was coming to a close. Although the boat was soon eclipsed by newer generations of submarine design, the Requin remained in service until 1968. Four years later, a non-profit organization brought it to Tampa and docked it at the downtown convention center. Plagued by low attendance, tours were discontinued in 1986. A contemporary account described the Requin as wallowing in the Hillsborough River like an old tin can. One city's tin is another city's treasure. In 1990, the sub was overhauled and carried by barge up the Mississippi River to a site on the Ohio River in Pittsburgh. The Carnegie Science Center proudly maintains the Requin. Again, hopefully Tampa will do so with the SS American Victory.

SS American Victory

When The Florida Aquarium opened in 1995 I was a little apprehensive about the Florida title. After all, wasn't this the state that hosts Sea World? Could our fish tank muscle its way between the glass-bottom boats of Silver Springs and the kitschy mermaids at Weeki Wachee? How about St. Augustine's venerable Marineland, forever linked with "The Creature from the Black Lagoon?"

I needn't worry. There was no need for hoop-jumping dolphins. The entire building was conceived to allow the visitor to follow a drop of water through the entire state's ecosystem. A glass and steel, scalloped shaped roof caps a gigantic terrarium that allows wading birds, such as herons and spoonbills, to mingle with visitors. Further along, you drift under bridges and wend your way through the aquifer on your way to the offshore reefs. The aquarium also is a research facility and examples of studies are displayed throughout the tour. There are few things our family of four have ever held in agreement, but the Florida Aquarium is one we all heartily enjoyed. For several years we took full advantage of our annual family passes. I found it particularly sweet that our daughter started giving the fish names until she started calling all the very ugliest ones, Charley.

The Florida Aquarium

Maybe I've watched too many old movies but I find Tampa Union Station a transcendental experience that puts me into a different era. The station has an additional trick up its sleeve, a lofty, ceilinged lobby that appears too large to fit inside the pragmatic, brick building. Union Station was built in 1912 to operate as an independent company. Two rail lines, the Seaboard Air Line and the Atlantic Coast Line, formerly Henry Plant's rail system, brought travelers from across the country. From the day it opened during World War I it was the first building most newcomers to Tampa would see.

After the war, air and automobile travel took huge bites out of rail traffic. Railroads valiantly fought back, streamlining their trains and anointing them with inspired names such as Silver Meteor and West Coast Champion, but to little avail. In 1971, the lines consolidated into Amtrak's holdings. In 1984, Amtrak closed the grand station and moved operations into a small, portable building beside the tracks. Thankfully, the non-profit Friends of Union Station in 1999 restored and reopened this romantic window into the past.

Reading about the Seaboard Air Line, a company formed before the first flights at Kitty Hawk, made me wonder if these guys envisioned trains lifted by hot air balloons or if our grandparents had been hoaxed, just as we were with promises of flying cars. It turns out that "airline" was just a promotional term for a railroad track that follows a straight line as it might be drawn in the air. Phooey.

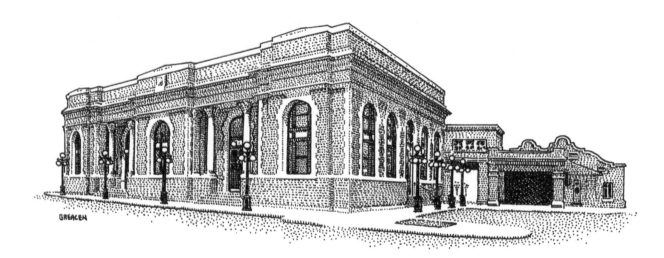

Tampa Union Station

Tampa grew up as a port city, but the cruise industry is a new game here. The port ships so much phosphate we could be called Phosphate City if only it had the alliteration of Cigar City. Henry Plant's use of cargo ships to transport troops from Tampa to Cuba during the Spanish-American War did little to foster the cruise business here. In the last decade or so, Tampa's Gulf side location has finally drawn some cruise ships away from their traditional Miami-area berths. Travelers driving across the Sunshine Skyway from Pinellas County to Manatee County may find it curious to be greeted to Hillsborough County as they cross this span. This navigational gerrymandering was carried out for the Port of Tampa to protect itself from the machinations of jealous, neighboring counties. The goal was to prevent building a bridge that might constrict shipping into Tampa Bay. When the present Sunshine Skyway Bridge opened in 1987 it seemed to allay any fears of interference to navigation. Cruising's popularity has, however, brought about a new generation of mega ships too tall to pass under the bridge. For all the gussying up with new terminal buildings, the Port of Tampa appears to be relegated to second-tier status. I addressed a solution a few years ago in my weekly cartoon in the Tampa Bay Times. As bigger ships head toward the bridge, passengers would assemble on one side. The resulting list would allow the ship to clear the span. I'm still waiting for a thank you.

Cruise Terminal 2

Sacred Heart Catholic Church has earned its place in the heart of Tampa. Its roots took hold in this sandy soil back when Tampa was just a small settlement standing in the shadow of the military outpost, Fort Brooke. Sacred Heart's first sanctuary was built in 1860 when the fort was in decline. It would be a long time before things got better. Exhausted by the Civil War, Tampa even gave up its city charter. Sacred Heart shared the misery and endured. Among the Tampa citizens lost to the yellow fever outbreak of 1888 were all three of the church's parish priests.

By 1905, things were looking up for Tampa and for the city's Catholic parish. The present granite and marble edifice was consecrated with great ceremony.Residents of all faiths were dazzled by its 135-foot dome and its prominent rose window, lit with stained glass crafted in Munich, Germany. At this time the church became known as Sacred Heart.

Previously the parish was inauspiciously named St. Luis Parish, in honor of Father Luis de Cancer. This Dominican priest had come to the shores of Tampa Bay in 1549, planning to minister to its Native Americans. Unfortunately, the previous two fellow Spaniards the natives met, Hernando de Soto and Panfilio Narvaez, displayed such brutality they left a bad taste in their mouths. Friar Cancer was clubbed to death as he waded ashore.

Sacred Heart Catholic Church

This building was home to a Glendale Federal Savings and Loan, now Northern Trust savings institution, change to Glendale Federal Savings and Loan, now Northern Trust savings institution, but I thought it was something dreamed up by Walt Disney. The institution looked like it had just escaped from Colonial Williamsburg. At the time, Tampa was topping its first real skyscraper and more would soon follow. Each new project seemed to be more generic than the last. The "beer can" building on the Hillsborough River was a refreshing exception. Glendale's building was one of the few that didn't attempt to blind you with all the sunlight bouncing off it. If I were in charge of downtown development I'd apply my "Glendale" plan. (Never mind that the business has changed hands and names.)

Each new project would have to pick a different genre for its exterior. Picture how uplifting it would be to walk from pagoda to ziggurat by way of basilica and citadel. Unfortunately, once again, they just don't listen to me.

Northern Trust

Early in the Spring of 1980, strategically placed explosives reduced the 68-year old Bay View Hotel into a pile of rubble and a cloud of dust. The demolition was delayed for about two hours to allow a fog to lift so that V.I.P.'s on the top of the First National Bank Building, then Tampa's tallest, could enjoy a bird's eye view.

Thus go we all.

It's obvious I love museums. I'm embarrassed it took me so long to figure out a way to make museum visits my job. The Tampa Bay History Center, the museum that pays homage to my adopted city, earns that love many times over. I also have been married for decades to Mary Denise, a former Tampa Tribune food writer/restaurant reviewer. The TBHC earns extra credit in that category. Too many museums view a food concession as merely a convenience or a profit source.

Rare is the memorable, museum-eating experience. TBHC's Columbia Cafe is a notable exception, deeply ingrained in the community. Columbia Restaurant Group president Richard Gonzmart is a Tampa food ways curator. Ybor City's Columbia Restaurant, the group's flagship, is Florida's oldest, family-owned restaurant. Cafe guests can sample many of the Cuban/Spanish dishes that help give this city its singular flavor. Back among the exhibits, the area's diverse cast of characters from Calusas to Cubans, railroaders to Rough Riders, are at the museum. The 2018 conquistadors, pirates and shipwrecks exhibit, called "Treasure Seekers" captures the attention of the most jaded teenager.

There are about 816,000 cars in the county. No figures exist for the number that bring tourists here. On display is a replica of the first car to roam Tampa, a shiny Curved Dash 1902 Oldsmobile. Inventor Ransom Olds enjoyed numerous connections with our area, including the creation of Oldsmar, at the top of Tampa Bay. Dig deeper and you will discover the car is No. 3. Enterprising bicycle owner Fred Ferman built two autos in 1899. He became friends with Ransom and opened a showroom that became one of the nation's oldest, continuously running dealerships.

Tampa Bay History Center

Tampa and St. Petersburg have always behaved right neighborly. A little rivalry might show up from time to time, but always good naturedly so. Then along came the question, where should the Tampa Bay Rays build their next stadium? Who knew cities could indulge in cat fights? The question remains unresolved even though the solution is right here. It began as a quip I made about turning the Hyde Park Mens' Club's imaginary barge into a floating ballfield. About a week later, I had a looming newspaper deadline and no other cartoon ideas, so the cross-bay stadium concept was born. When the cartoon was printed in the local Tampa Bay Times, the resulting groundswell was, in a word, underwhelming. Still, I was infatuated with the idea and couldn't let it go. Soon after I ran into both mayors at parties in their respective cities and pitched them ardently. Yes there was a cash bar, so it wasn't the alcohol talking, at least in St. Petersburg.

Surprisingly, both mayors appear to have misplaced my telephone number or business cards. They never got to hear about my nearly-patented, telescoping stabilizers that assure the only pitching will happen between the mound and home plate. Until a site is finally selected, the trans-bay field isn't dead. Just the opposite, everyday it becomes more and more relevant. More powerful hurricanes? How about the power to move out of harm's way. Sea level rise? See how we rise to the challenge? Call me.

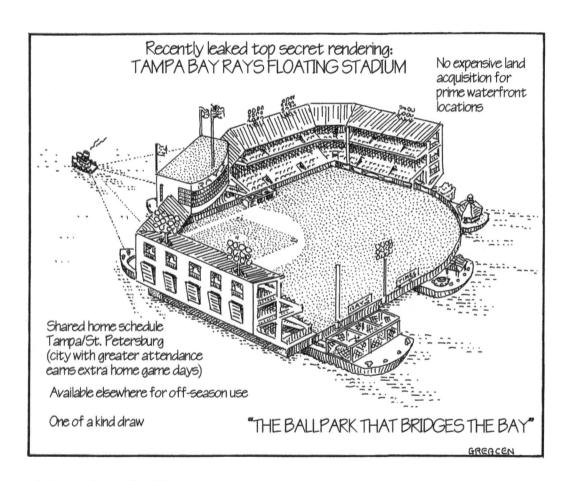

Cartoon in Tampa Bay Times

YBOR CITY

Centro Asturiano de Tampa was an aristocrat among Tampa's cigar worker mutual aid societies. With membership based on family roots tracing back to the Asturias region of Spain, the club exhibited a certain snob appeal. This ambitious organization even boasted its own hospital and cemetery. Even today when the club's place in society has faded, Asturias pride is on full display at its well maintained headquarters. When the club's first building was destroyed by fire in 1910, the Centro aspired to replace it with the grandest clubhouse in the city. The society hired M. Leo Elliot, considered the dean of Tampa architecture, to design its new showcase. All of the expected amenities: ballroom, theater, cantina, library and gym, were included in the new clubhouse. The club claims its bar, perhaps the building's crowning piece of ostentation, is the largest, onyx bar in the world.

Today, company health plans and mass media have lessened the importance of Tampa's mutual aid societies. The Centro Asturiano has pivoted into the new reality by renting its space for events of all kinds. I have attended holiday parties, weddings, award ceremonies and celebrations of all sorts in this grand old edifice. I'm proud to cross "have a drink at the world's largest onyx bar" off my bucket list.

Centro Asturiano de Tampa

The Circulo Cubano, or as it is better known The Cuban Club, shares most of the attributes of fellow Ybor City mutual aid societies with an extra dose of passion. The club's Cuban, ex-pat membership would bring throngs to hear revolutionary Jose Marti when he canvassed for support for insurrection against Cuba's Spanish rule. Legend has it the club thwarted an attempt by Spanish agents to poison Marti when he spoke here. The passion also has applied to music; Celia Cruz, Glenn Miller and Tommy Dorsey drew huge audiences.

The vast building's theatricality was not lost on Charles Todd "Bud" Lee, Tampa's Pied Piper of the arts in the '70s. Bud had recently walked away from a highly-celebrated, photography career that had spanned the nation and beyond. His photography was in Esquire, Vogue, Rolling Stone, Harper's Bazaar, The New York Times and Town & Country. Through a grant from the National Endowment for the Arts, he established himself locally as Artist-Filmmaker in the Schools. Bud's real genius was promoting the artistry of others and he struck gold.

The decline of Tampa's cigar industry had hollowed out Ybor City. Low rents and exotic architecture lured artists like a magnet. Bud would discover a colony of painters, potters, sculptors, glass workers and printmakers, who rarely worked in unison. Bud changed that.

Ybor City's Artists and Writers Balls are a lasting testimony to his unique skills. Most artists are incapable of forming a one-car parade but under Bud's wonderful, hands-free, guidance, Ybor's creative community staged celebrations that were a marvel. Several venues were used but the Cuban Club hosted the best. The "Daughters of Bizarro," "Bad Taste in Outer Space," "Children of Paradise," "The Disney Dali Ball" and "Calhoun's Little Hawaiian Circus for the Poor," balls drew revelers in eye-popping costumes. Crowds stuffed the cavernous Cuban Club's four floors and courtyard. The balls initially spoofed on Tampa's high society gatherings but then the spoofees ended up happily joining the festivities. It was at one of these galas that I learned a cardinal rule for costume; dress comfortably. I lit on the cartoon metaphor of a guy who had lost it all, reduced to wearing a barrel. It just so happened I knew where I could get my hands on a barrel. What could go wrong? That turned out to be a really good idea - for 15 minutes of what became a long, long, long, weary night.

The Cuban Club

The German-American Club was one of the many mutual aid societies that served the Ybor City and West Tampa cigar manufacturing community. In its heyday, cigar making was highly stratified with different ethnic groups designated to specific tasks. German immigrants served in the lithography shops that created the ornate graphics for cigar boxes. For many around the world their only impression of Tampa was through the images that adorned those boxes. The story of this building is ladened with irony. The 1909 building included a theater, swimming pool and a bowling alley. Although it was formed by and for German Americans, it was the only one of the clubs open to all ethnic groups. That liberality didn't shield the club from the surge of anti-German sentiment brought on by the sinking of the RMS Lusitania ocean liner and World War I. In 1918, after vandals damaged the clubhouse interior, the shuttered building was sold. Adding to the irony is that many founders were prominent members of Tampa's Jewish community, including the Maas family, owners of Maas Brothers department stores, and four-term mayor Herman Glogowski (the only mayor to serve four non-consecutive terms). The spirit of inclusiveness still resides in the building, which now houses LGBTQ-friendly health services.

The German-American Club

Although the initial wave of immigrants that worked in Ybor City's cigar factories were Cubans and Spaniards traveling by way of Cuba, the Italians were close behind. Word of the comparatively good life Sicilians found in the Tampa area spread back home, enticing more relatives to travel here. Although they were offered admission in some of the other social clubs, the newcomers created the formidable L'Unione Italiana, or as it's better known, The Italian Club. When the first clubhouse burned in 1912, it was replaced by the present structure in 1918. Designed by M. Leo Elliott, the structure pays homage to Sicily's Greco-Roman heritage. As with the other clubs members could enjoy theater, bowling, ballroom dancing and more. The Italian Club has been successful in surviving Ybor City's suburban flight and the changing needs of members. The club has adapted well to serving as a venue for various social events and its members continue to bolster the club. The organization is not shy about its lengthy list of members: mayors, city council members, county commissioners and judges. It does, however, give a little less play to a successful businessman and known Mafia boss in its ranks, Santo Trafficante Sr.

The Italian Club of Tampa

I usually try to avoid being too harsh or judgmental when it comes to old buildings but I can't help myself here; the old El Centro Espanol de Tampa Casino in Ybor City has been reduced to the status of "picture pony," the one, authentic edifice in a modern, lookalike complex. It's like the times when children wear straw hats and pose on diminutive horses while a photographer turns them into cowgirls or cowboys. In 1912, the Centro's members hired architect Francis Kennard
to build a replacement for their outgrown clubhouse. This was an era when the area's social clubs and mutual-aid societies were trying to outdo each other. These buildings were crafted to last forever; unfortunately, their mission was not.

The children of Ybor's original, immigrant population wouldn't need the clubs to fit in, but ethnic pride enabled some to carry on. Others became relics. After a long period of benign neglect, Ybor City caught the attention of developers who saw the potential of marketing a New Orleans-style French Quarter entertainment district. In 2000, Centro Ybor was plopped in the center of the neighborhood. A 20-screen movie theater, restaurants, souvenir shops and bars were wrapped in a pseudo-Spanish, revival look. To give the project a whiff of authenticity, the restored El Centro Espanol building was preserved (almost pickled) in the heart of the complex. The building is a gem and the restaurant it housed was interesting but I sorely miss the Don Quixote Cafe, a quirky basement-level bistro that served traditional Cuban fare spiked with force-field doses of garlic. The restaurant, and the artists and writers who frequented it, vanished in the wave of tourism. You can read some vivid accounts of those times in my friend Paul Wilborn's "Cigar City: Tales From a 1980s Creative Ghetto."
(St. Petersburg Press)

The Casino Theatre

The Seidenberg Cigar Company is a perfect snapshot of the amazing rise-and-fall of the American cigar industry. The failed Cuban insurrection of 1868 compelled Samuel Seidenberg to join fellow cigar manufacturers to move two factories from Havana, Cuba to Key West. Although Seidenberg initially resisted joining the next mass migration of his cronies from Key West to Tampa Bay's Ybor City, he finally made the move in 1895.

Although Ybor City and West Tampa had the impressive tally of at least 150 cigar factories operating then, it pays to put this number into perspective. In 1895, there were approximately 42,000 cigar factories throughout the U.S. Around Central Florida, smaller cities such as Bradenton, Bartow, and Sarasota were making their own cigar brands. The critical difference was the scale of production. Unlike the massive fortresses built in and around Ybor City, most factories consisted of a handful of rollers, working out of storefronts or even private homes. When cigar popularity waned, some cities were left with vacant fossils of the industry. The Seidenberg factory served as a warehouse for a number of years. In 1994, it was converted into the Ybor City Brewing Company. Engineering and technology firms have replaced that. For one company's ribbon-cutting ceremony, I made a giant, 4-by-6-foot, paper cigar band. Seidenberg's brands, by the way, were La Rosa Española and Buffos cigars. It has been a dozen years since I last smoked a cigar but I'd light one up right now if someone handed over a Buffo.

Seidenberg Cigar Company

Having put his name on Tampa's new cigar-making community, it's no surprise Vicente de Ybor went on to build its Alpha factory in 1886. Ybor's complex was the largest cigar factory in the world. The warehouse, stemmery and water tower, as well as the main building that accommodated 600 skilled rollers, took up a full city block. Just as one day Henry Ford's River Rouge plant would take in raw steel and crank out Model Ts, Ybor's operation brought Cuban tobacco directly from the docks on its own rail track and shipped many boxes of his world famous Prince of Wales-brand stogies. Having brokered the land deal between Tampa's city officials and his fellow cigarmakers, Ybor naturally got first pick for locating his factory. He astutely picked one of the highest points in the parcel and its cupola atop his central building has lorded over the neighborhood ever since.

Today, the former factory is known as Ybor Square, a name it was given when it was redeveloped in 1972. Publisher and businessman Harris Mullen saw the potential for this empty, but totally intact, relic as a tourist site. For the next quarter century, antique stores, gift shops and restaurants such as Rough Riders brought people back to Ybor City. After another makeover, the complex is owned by the Church of Scientology and curiosity spurred me to stop in and take a peek. In one corner there was office space set aside for L. Ron Hubbard's exclusive use. Nobody appreciates my humor; I told them that L. Ron had informed me he wasn't coming in that day and I was welcome to use the space.

Ybor Square

Ybor City's Labor Temple, AKA The Castle, is a colorful building that has lived two different lives. During its first stage as a labor hall, it was a lightning rod for strife. It is pleasant to picture rows of happy workers hand rolling cigars while lectors read current events and popular literature for their entertainment. The reality is more contentious. The major cigar makers originally built their factories in Ybor City hoping to escape the labor unrest that had followed them from Havana to Key West. The Labor Temple was built in 1925 to oppose the united front of the factory owners and 1931 was the high-water mark of violence. Factory owners sought the help of the KKK and jailing, along with deportations, was widespread. Unrest only ended when mechanization and changing smoking trends eliminated most of the jobs.

By the late '80s, developers recognized the potential of the neighborhood as an entertainment mecca. Tucked off the main strip at Seventh Avenue, the Labor Temple, now The Castle bar and multilevel dance club, developed its own singular style. The medieval look inside and out became a natural draw for the goth set. The Castle assumed a "be what you want to be" air. Walking through the door you would be justified in thinking you had entered a Comic Con event. Among its unique features is a "moat," water coursing through the bar top's perimeter. When I recognize something floating by that I've seen before, it is time to finish my drink and head home.

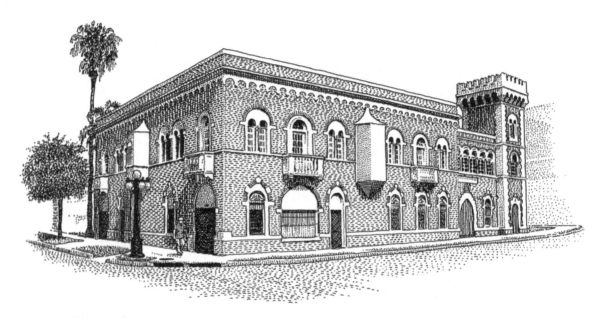

The Castle

The Ybor City State Museum preserved three early casitas (little houses) next to its gardens because these humble abodes were the glue that held Ybor City and West Tampa together. Almost every acre of those neighborhoods, which wasn't taken up by the cigar factories or business establishments, was blanketed with these shotgun houses. Amenities were pretty basic and air conditioning was unheard of; most relied on outhouses. All had front porches that helped turn strangers into neighbors. The employees who came to work at the factories were a mobile group with few or no bonds of company loyalty.

Vincente de Ybor wisely made casitas an incentive to stay. Departing from the old factory town model of total ownership, Ybor constructed houses and sold them to workers at cost. The whisper of better wages elsewhere, homesickness and wanderlust, were less likely to undercut a labor force that had a stake in the new community.

As a testimony to their durability, many casitas remain in use today as homes or repurposed as shops and offices. As an acknowledgement of their primitive carpentry properties where they previously stood are meccas for metal detector hobbyists. Over the years, the less-than-perfect flooring let plenty of loose change drop under the little buildings.

Ybor City Casitas

With the exception of Bern's Steak House, strip clubs, and Tom Brady and the Buccaneers winning the Super Bowl in Tampa, it seems all the things Tampa is known for start in Ybor City: Cuban cigars, Cuban sandwiches and Cuban bread. Two of those three feature long crusty loaves, made from flour, yeast and lard, which is why the Ferlita Bakery was the perfect home to the Ybor City State Museum.

In 1896, Francisco Ferlita lit his bakery's first ovens. His family kept creating edible delights until 1973. The brick building occupied by the museum was built in 1923, replacing the original, which burned the year before. To stay ahead of the competition, Ferlita offered home delivery. The original horse and buggy gave way to delivery trucks, a service that remained until the day the bakery permanently closed. The expression "museum ready" could have been coined for the Ferlita Building. The same year the bakery closed, it launched into its new occupation as an interpreter of Ybor's history.

Jimmy Reader, my brother-in-law, earned a footnote in the Ferlita heritage. In the late '80s he opened the Ferlita-Reader Bakery with one of Francisco's descendants. The wholesale bakery, based in Brandon, lasted about four years. Jimmy asked me to draw a little cartoon baker for his business card but I created the art shown on the right instead.

Ferlita Bakery

You could write a few books about favorite restaurants that have come and gone in Ybor City. Las Novedades, Cafe Mercedes, Rough Riders, Cafe Creole, The Silver Ring, Spanish Park and La Tropicana, for starters, would make compelling chapters in such a compilation. Or, you could write one book on the one that survived, the Columbia Restaurant. Too late, though, as Andrew Huse aptly chronicled this Tampa treasure in his "The Columbia, Celebrating a Century of History, Culture and Cuisine."

This venerable restaurant now overseen by Richard Gonzmart, its founders' great-grandson, prides itself for plenty of "olds" including oldest restaurant in Florida and oldest Spanish restaurant in the U.S. You would be hard pressed to locate someone living in Tampa who hadn't attended a birthday, wedding, reunion, memorial service, political campaign, going up-the-river-send off, or some kind of life passage, in this city's icon. This drawing appears in a full-color format on coffee mugs sold in Columbia's souvenir shop. When I met with the store buyer, she cut my pitch short and handed me a postcard that had this view. She laconically stated, "draw this and I will buy your mugs." Business is business and she has been good to her word, but what makes my day is hearing the shop manager exclaim, "Oh boy, mugs!" each and every time I make another delivery.

The Columbia Restaurant

Las Novedades has burned, moved, sold, then finally closed, but it still has a large hold on Ybor City's heart. Restaurateur Manuel Menendez opened the cafe in 1890. Las Novedades had three owners named Manuel, which would be the blueprint for all of Tampa's Spanish-style restaurants. Its name, which means new or novelty, is fitting as the cafe earned fame as the site of the "Charge of the Yellow Rice Brigade." Tampa at the time was the mustering place for the forces embarking to Cuba for the Spanish-American War. A rowdy and bored troop of Teddy Roosevelt's Rough Riders rode their mounts into the restaurant and demanded food. A wise Menendez complied and served the soldiers drinks, knowing they would bring him priceless publicity. In 1946, Las Novedades moved to the corner location with its iconic Moorish tower. The venerated name came down from the building in 1972. When I moved to Tampa the following year, a New York-based chain operated a Steak and Brew restaurant there. It only lasted three years, but the free beer and wine with dinner policy lured me more than a few times. Several nightclubs followed. El Goya received the most attention with its flamboyant, cross-dressing entertainers. Today, a newly built boutique hotel has appended itself onto the old restaurant building. Haya, named for one of the pioneer cigar makers, honors the Las Novedades hospitality tradition.

Las Novedades

Cephas Gilbert recently closed his eponymous restaurant (I know, you thought it was Jamaican) after a 38-year run. It is appropriate he is included in this illustration because the colorful spot is all about Cephas. Gilbert left his native Jamaica at the age of 17 and traveled the world as a merchant mariner for 13 years. When he settled in Tampa, he went about turning a parcel of Ybor City's industrial fringe into a home away from home. He served his native specialties in his restaurant, Cephas Hot Shop, and hosted reggae bands in an outdoor amphitheater. Midway through the restaurant's run a fire stopped Cephas' in its tracks. There was no insurance to pay for repairs but karma stepped in. Josh Doering, a loyal customer, began a Go Fund Me campaign. The effort was supercharged by the arrival of movie producer Brad Furman. He was scouting the area for the Tampa-based movie, "The Infiltrator," fell in love with Gilbert's site and used it in multiple scenes. Those rental fees put Cephas' back in business. Most recently, Gilbert is focused on selling his Aloe Vera health drinks and dispensing longevity advice. He opened a booth on Ybor's main commercial strip where he will continue promoting health, one body at a time. Cephas and I are the same age and I will be interested to see who retires first.

Cephas Hot Shop

Among Ybor City buildings, the El Pasaje is a contender that has worn the most hats. In its storied career the building has been a hotel, restaurant, speakeasy, business office, social club, newspaper office, military recruiting station and more. Said to be a copy of a similarly named building in Havana, Cuba, the Pasaje was built in 1886 and originally served as an office for Vicente de Ybor's various investments. Pasaje, Spanish for passage, refers to the Havana building's use as a safe house for anti-colonial agitators. Cuban revolutionary Jose Marti conspicuously used Ybor City's El Pasaje to canvas for funds to support the Cuban rebels. In the early 20th Century, the building became the El Pasaje Hotel and home to the Cherokee Club, a social organization for influential businessmen. The hotel's register included such guests as President Grover Cleveland, Sir Winston Churchill and Frederick Remington. Every Florida governor, from 1890 to 1935, came to the El Pasaje restaurant to glad-hand constituents. Some of my favorite times were spent there. Anthony D'Avanza Jr. applied his Louisiana culinary talents to shrimp Creole, seafood gumbo and spicy crawfish when this was home to his long-running Cafe Creole. Paul and Sally Hooper's Cajun Connection had us dancing in the courtyard to performances by favorite bands such as Michael Doucet's BeauSoleil, one of the best Cajun bands in the world, and the Hot Summer Nights. The historical marker on the building must have run out of room because it fails to note that I (as a notary) performed my first wedding ceremony here for some close friends, fellow journalists from The Tampa Tribune and WTVT-TV.

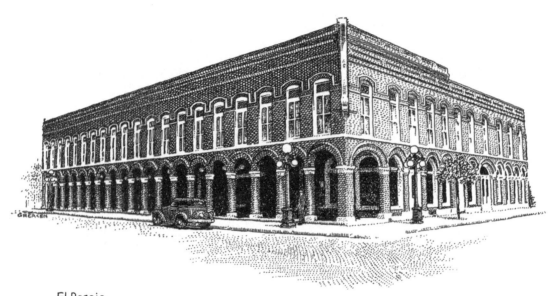

El Pasaje

I have several friends born at The Don Vicente. In a broader sense it could be said Ybor City was born there, too. It was built in 1895 for the architects and real estate agents who designed the neighborhood from scratch. Tampa's city fathers offered cigar manufacturers an adjacent parcel of land that was essentially a blank slate. In 1903, the building assumed its second career as home to El Buen Publico Clinic, a role it would fill for the next 70 years. Many Ybor natives trace their beginnings to the facility.

After its closure the building would sit empty until one of those natives, developer Jack Shiver, bought it in 1998 and made it his pet project. Shiver converted the old clinic into a luxury boutique hotel. The decor of the 16-room lodging reflected the glory days of old Ybor. I had the honor of performing two marriages in the hotel's elegant lobby. One of the most unusual I've performed was when friend Jody Klay asked me to officiate his niece's wedding. He somehow failed to inform me the theme was goth, as in dim candelabra lighting and all its attendants clad in mysterious, antiquated black attire. The limo was a shiny, stretch black hearse. I stood in the center of the ceremony wearing my three-button blazer, thinking about the long-tailed mourning jacket hanging in my closet. Maybe I'll get a second chance some day but it won't be at the Don Vicente. A few years ago the hotel was sold and converted into retail and office space.

The Don Vicente

It seems everybody remembers this Ybor City house set on the corner of Second Avenue and 23rd Street, yet nobody I ask can recall anything about it. Most of the prominent cigar manufacturing magnates felt no obligation to live among their employees but here was a successful individual staying loyal to the neighborhood. What could better encourage the American dream than this flamboyant residence set among the modest, shotgun-style houses surrounding it?

Sad proof that this home, along with much of the community, has seen better days is the half dozen or so mailboxes sheltered on the front porch.

Ybor Victorian house

DAVIS ISLANDS

Tampa holds a couple of coveted firsts in aviation history. Most notably, the first scheduled commercial airline operated between St. Petersburg and Tampa, beginning Jan. 1, 1914. Following World War II, the Army Air Corps established the first Strategic Air Command base at Tampa's MacDill Field. No less important, today the field is host to two of our military's Unified Commands. Back at the time of the first commercial flights there were no airports nearby, so fliers traveled from St. Pete's waterfront to Tampa's Hillsborough River using a Benoist airboat piloted by pioneering aviator Tony Jannus.

Tampa's first municipal airport, which was built on Davis Islands in 1935, included a seaplane basin that went largely unused. Within a decade, planes serving the airlines required more space than available on the island so it, now Tampa International Airport, moved six miles from downtown. The remaining facilities, now named after the man who gave the land to the city, Peter O. Knight, provides services for small planes. Its current terminal was built in the '60s, and its attempt to invoke an aircraft look is a nice try. A few times lately I've seen a small experimental aircraft fitted with pontoons doing touch-and-goes on Hillsborough Bay. On a most recent occasion, I had to calm down an extremely agitated passerby who was sure he had witnessed a horrible crash. Sadly, a 1916 plane crash into the Black Sea was the fate of Jannus, while working for pre Revolutionary Russia.

Peter O. Knight Airport

This is one of the original D.P. Davis homes on Davis Islands in South Tampa. Inspired by the Spanish, colonial-style homes the Meisner brothers built on South Florida's east coast, Davis built a handful of these fantasy houses before Tampa's real estate bubble burst. It enjoys a sweeping view of Hillsborough Bay and the Tampa peninsula. When our children were young, I offered house renderings as an auction item for St. John's Episcopal School's fundraising events. I was pleased when this was the home of the highest bidder. I was a little less pleased when I received a call from the owner, just after I'd delivered the finished art, telling me she had just asked her landscaper to cut down the tree in front of the house and wanted me to revise the drawing accordingly. Of course I obliged but I retained a digital version of the original for my files.

In another year, the high bidder at the school auction had me excited because her address was the location of our honeymoon cottage. I was in for a shock when I went over to take reference photos to find that our sweet, one-story first home had been plowed down to be replaced with a huge, hulking, "McMansion." I had to keep my thoughts to myself because the owner happened to be our son's fifth-grade teacher that year. That was then and this is now; nice looking house, my butt.

202 Riviera Avenue

D.P. Davis left Tampa with a distinctive community and an enduring mystery. Davis, the quintessential boom-time developer, rode the bubble right up to the brink of its burst, then vanished without a trace. The fact that his disappearance left his young widow, his mistress and many prominent members of the Tampa business community holding the bag, adds to the mystique. Davis' plan was to create an island neighborhood complete with its own shopping, yacht club, golf course and hospital, where there had only been spoil islands.

Fortunately, the main features of the project were in place when the crash came. Davis Islands survived as a waterside, suburban enclave just minutes from downtown. Its residential architecture is a blend of original '20s Mediterranean revival to post-modern, with lots of "Leave It To Beaver" ranch styles between. The Mirasol was a fashionable, seven-story hotel that opened just before the Florida boom went bust. Although it was converted into apartments, the Mirasol sacrificed little of its elegance. The front doesn't just face the street, it lords over the community's main approach Davis Boulevard. On the back, it intimately hugs the private boat basin. Davis Islands' tallest building at seven stories has 58 units, ranging from efficiencies to an opulent penthouse. One of these days I'm going to buy a lottery ticket so I can afford to rent that penthouse.

The Mirasol Apartments

Florida has played the role of trendsetter, though not always in a good way. When our nation became crippled by the 1929 stock market crash, Florida already was three years into its own self-inflicted depression. Although Miami is viewed as the perfect case study of overheated real estate speculation fed by willful self delusion, the Tampa Bay area was hardly innocent of this behavior. Just as Carl Fisher had dazzled the real estate world by transforming sea bottom into prime waterfront property in Miami, Tampa's D.P. Davis turned spoil islands at the mouth of the Hillsborough River into an exotic destination. The historic 1926 Palace of Florence, one of the crown jewels of Davis' masterpiece, was completed just as the bottom dropped out of the Florida boom time.

Designed by artist Athos Menaboni, the 28-unit apartments' towers, courtyard and external staircases are elements borrowed directly from the Italian city's town hall, Palazzo Vecchio. The regal flourishes belie the relatively modest proportions of many of the apartment units, a factor that allowed the Palace to survive the coming hard times relatively unscathed. Its current owner, Gaspar Properties Inc., made sure the building lives up to its original, boom time expectations.

The Palace's prominent position on Davis Boulevard made it an unofficial icon for Davis Islands. For me, it triggers a vision of the popular M.C. Escher engraving, "House of Stairs," which employs an optical illusion of a perpetually uphill staircase where the laws of gravity don't apply.

The Palace of Florence

MOSI, the Museum of Science and Industry, opened in 1982 in its current location, across Fowler Avenue from the University of South Florida campus. It had its start 20 years before as a collection of local fauna, flora, and geological specimens housed in some cabins set along the Hillsborough River in Sulphur Springs. By 1996, MOSI had grown into the largest science museum in the Southeast, having added a public library, a planetarium, and the IMAX Dome Theatre shown here.

Unfortunately, as of this writing, 85 percent of the museum has been mothballed. Its long-term plan is to relocate downtown among the city's other museums. Developers already have dreams and schemes for the Fowler Avenue property. I'd love to see the IMAX Dome Theatre left in place, possibly repurposed as a pool hall or pinball parlor. When our daughter, Alexandra, was between three and four I took her and her friend Jenny up to MOSI to see a traveling exhibit of full-scale, automated dinosaurs. After walking three or four strides into the display I realized the girls weren't by my side. Looking back, I saw them by the entrance frozen in their tracks. Their eyes were the size of saucers. On the way home I enjoyed listening to them, recapping their adventure, especially when I heard Alexandra inform her pal, "Daddy didn't know they were real."

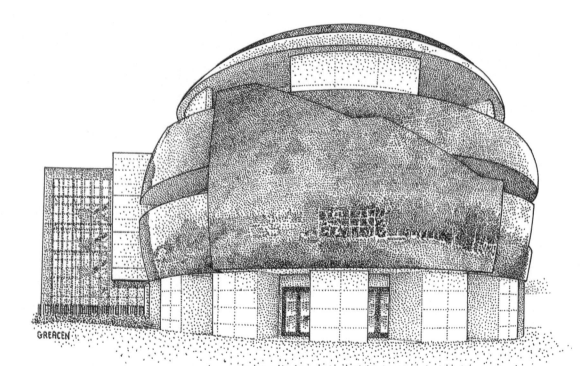

IMAX Dome Theatre at MOSI

MOSI hosted an annual fundraising event called Einstein Food & Wine, the brainchild of friends Rob and Sadie Pariseau. Wine merchants and local restaurants set up sampling booths among the museum's exhibits. Live music and free cigars were additional perks. My wife Mary Denise covered the event for The Tampa Tribune and brought me along to take photographs. One of the cigars given out came in a particularly handsome wood box. It obviously was a premium cigar because guests were snapping them up. I asked the representative for one of the empty boxes and he readily obliged.

While I was working my way through the crowd to find my wife, I was approached by a nondescript guy who directed my attention to a gorgeous, fashionably dressed woman. He said, "She doesn't usually do this sort of thing but she's interested in meeting you." I'm not really smart, but I am realistic. At this stage in my life, if I was to succumb to the advances of an attractive woman, the most likely outcome would be waking up in a strange bathtub full of ice missing a kidney. I told the fellow I ought to check with my wife first and left. As I walked around my ego was still flying high until I looked down at the box in my hand. It hit me that it wasn't me she wanted to meet, it was the big spender who caught her eye who thought nothing of buying a box of the most pricey cigars in the house.

MOSI Recyclosaurus

While digital reading may one day completely replace printed books, I guarantee it won't happen in my lifetime. I know other like-minded souls to confidently agree. Sadly, Tampa's Inkwood Books, our last independent bookseller, isn't around. My neighbor Leslie Reiner, along with Carla Jimenez, opened Inkwood in 1991 and in 2013 sold it to one of their best customers, Stefani Beddingfield. In 2017, Beddingfield moved the store from its South Tampa location to downtown but the transplant failed to thrive. Book lovers were left with a good news/bad news scenario when she closed Inkwood in 2019. The good news: Stefani's sister Julia owns a prospering Inkwood Books outlet. The bad news: it's in Haddonfield, N. J., near my Merchantville, N.J., hometown. Over the years Tampa's Inkwood Books cultivated many new customers through author talks and book signings.

Mary Denise and I stopped by the store years ago to listen to our friend, former Tampa Tribune journalist, Tim Dorsey. Dorsey has a loyal following for his 25 books featuring Serge A. Storms, Coleman and other crazy cronies.

As luck would have it, he was in the middle of describing his first meeting with his future father-in-law. As they struggled to size each other up the dad asked Tim, "I trust you are going to have a priest perform the wedding." Tim's answer, "No, a cartoonist." From that point forward, they understood each other. I was that cartoonist. I'm also a notary, empowered to wed folks in Florida. At the wedding, the dad was as charming as one could be.

Inkwood Books

The Jose Gaspar Pirate Ship is the centerpiece of Tampa's biggest civic celebration, the Gasparilla Pirate Invasion and Parade. If the city ever decides it needs a slogan for this, I offer "Putting Racy into Piracy." Miss Louise Francis Dodge, society editor of The Tampa Tribune took some liberties with West Coast Florida history and gave new life to a legend about a charismatic buccaneer. The town adopted a pirate theme in 1904 for its annual May Day parade. Wealthy citizens showed off their new play things, horseless carriages, by decorating them to put into the parade. By 1911, the novelty wore off, so they rented a schooner and staged an invasion to spice up the parade. The Jose Gaspar ship, built in Tampa's shipyard in 1954, was for the sole purpose of being loaded up with costumed pirates and getting towed to the downtown waterfront with more than a thousand watercraft in its wake.

For many years the ensuing parade acted as an elaborate Pied Piper, leading children up to the entrance of the Florida State Fairgrounds on opening day. Jose Gaspar was one of the most romantic pirates that never existed. Legend has him living and looting off the Gulf Coast from the late 1700s to 1821. No document to support the legend has ever shown up. There was brief hope when Juan Gomez came forward, claiming to have been Gaspar's cabin boy. This colorful trapper and fishing guide from Panther Key wove tales of this connection but wasn't content to leave it there. He stretched his birth date back to 1776 and garnished his biography with fighting the Seminoles, gun running in Cuba, greeting Napoleon, and sharing cigars with General Grant. That has never been enough to rain on a good Gasparilla parade.

Jose Gaspar Pirate Ship

The University of Tampa has experienced remarkable growth during the last four decades and I'm proud to have documented with my pen and ink some of the progress.

Because the university has been on such a tear, I've occasionally been called to produce a rendering using nothing but the architects' initial elevations. In other instances, I've been asked to draw buildings on campus that sit where earlier ones I'd drawn used to be. It was a nice acknowledgment of my work when the university president's wife asked me for a pen-and-ink treatment of their new home. Our city is really a small town, as I knew the house's previous owners even though the home is not in my neighborhood. The university's first lady wrote a gracious note saying she really liked my drawing.

My art hasn't always had that effect on her husband. Over the course of the 17 years my cartoons ran in the Tampa Bay Times, "Tampa U" has sometimes been a backdrop or even the subject of those panels. Such was the case when the school added lacrosse fields. Somehow it escaped the planners' attention that the fields' orientation and proximity to one of Tampa's busiest streets created a liability. The school quickly bandaged that by hanging an enormous net. My next week's cartoon showed two groundskeepers trying to figure out what to do with the small plane caught in the web. A friend of mine who works at the university relayed that the president used some choice words about my cartoon. You can't please everyone.

405 S. Manhattan Avenue

The University of South Florida has had an amazing run. In 1956, it was nothing but a charter and an abandoned World War II airfield. By the early '70s, the university had grown to a substantial campus, although it was still considered a commuter school. Today, with 14 colleges, 180 majors, high-profile sports teams, and three campuses, the University of South Florida is the state's fourth-largest institution of higher education. Go Bulls.

It hasn't always been smooth sailing for the Bulls' logo. USF originally adopted the brahman bull for the school's mascot. These Asian imports, well-suited for South Florida's heat and intermittent drought, could be seen grazing in fields around the campus. What looks good out in a pasture doesn't always translate well onto sportswear and these humpback cows didn't instill pride or awe in their competitors. Even put into a boxing stance the Golden Brahman looked like the hunchbacked child of Notre Dame's fighting Irishman and University of Florida's fighting Gator. Cooler heads eventually morphed the mascot into a more mainstream bull and the identity crisis abated. The monogram that subtly turned the USF "U" into a stylized bull's head should have finished the issue for good. Just a few years ago, however, someone mucked with the brand and a new logo that narrowly escaped an infringement suit from Merrill Lynch, was rammed through. After eight months of campus-wide scorn and more than $100,000 squandered on the redo, the horned U is back. Go Bulls.

USF Marshall Student Center

When I refer to Thomas R. Robinson High School as a newer school it's not because it has that new school smell; it's a relative thing. Robinson is more than 60-years old, yet many of its neighboring public schools are centenarians. Enjoy this drawing because changes are in the works for a completely new campus. Unlike its older brethren, which assumed the look of antique, architectural styles, Robinson adheres to Frank Lloyd Wright's modern canon, form follows function. The school was built to serve newly developed neighborhoods, setting up a rivalry with nearby Plant High School. This rivalry became characterized as the old guard vs. the new.

Over the years, fluctuations caused the boundary between these schools to shift, often putting Knights and Panthers families loyalties to test. In 2006, Robinson became host to an International Baccalaureate program. Its inevitable graduates will go on to bring fame and prestige to the school through their achievements. That can't happen soon enough. Currently, four of the school's best-known alumni are on television: wrestlers, not that there's anything wrong with that. Somehow, though, the motto "Home of Hulkamania" doesn't translate into Latin very well.

Robinson High School

South Tampa's H.B. Plant High School is yet another entity named for the entrepreneur that connected this city to the world with rails. Plant High opened in 1927 and has grown to accommodate an enrollment of more than 2,500 students today. In spite of Florida's transient demographic, Plant enjoys a strong multigenerational loyalty. My own family includes three generations of proud Plant Panthers. This tradition has led to extraordinary alumni support. That support helps explain Plant High's consistent rating as one of the best public schools in Florida and academic "A" rating.

Plant has a sizable list of accomplished graduates. Stephen Stills of Crosby, Stills, Nash, and Young, the comedian Gallagher and baseball's Wade Boggs are among the most prominent. At least five of my son Scott's Panther football teammates have gone on to play in the National Football League. My wife Mary Denise's class of 1968 is a favorite example of the school's cohesiveness. Waiting five years to gather at reunions is way too long to endure. Her reunion committee often plans birthday celebrations and several interval events, just to enjoy each other.

H.B. Plant High School

Hillsborough High School holds the honor of being the oldest public high school in Tampa, as well as all of Hillsborough County. It enrolled its first students in 1882. The present building, its distinctive Gothic architecture designed by Francis Kennard, opened in 1928. Kennard also created the plans for some of Ybor City's palatial social clubs. In 1931, the fledgling University of Tampa shared space here before moving into the former Tampa Bay Hotel. Hillsborough High is one of four schools in Hillsborough County to have been bestowed an International Baccalaureate program. Among the many achievers who graduated from the school include Major League Baseball's Gary Sheffield and Dwight "Doc" Gooden. Country singer Slim Whitman probably polished his yodeling skills in the halls. Anyone who has ever been spoon-fed from a jar of Gerber's baby food has looked upon the face of alumna Ann Turner Cook, the original Gerber Baby.

When I moved here I discovered the Plant High vs. Hillsborough High rivalry, which at that time was only slightly less intense than the Hatfields' and McCoys' enmity. I have worked hard to not take sides in spite of marrying into a multi-generational Plant family.

There is one point about Hillsborough High that I can't avoid criticizing, its choice of mascots. These guys were the first school in town, which gave them the first pick of a ferocious animal or fearsome warrior.

What did they pick? A terrier. Woof.

Hillsborough High School

Looking at the stately campus of the Academy of the Holy Names on Bayshore Boulevard, it is hard to imagine what the two nuns who planted its seed would think today. The pair of Sisters of the Holy Names, who came from Key West in 1881, would have seen very little that would foreshadow the dynamic growth of the city or the school. Beginning in a two-room schoolhouse, the academy had its work cut out just surviving outbreaks of yellow fever and regional, financial setbacks. Tenaciously, the school not only survived but moved to progressively larger facilities. Any questions regarding its future were put to rest in 1928 when the cornerstone of the current Bayshore site was laid.

The same academy that once fit in that two-room building now enrolls about 1,000 girls and boys in pre-kindergarten through 8th grade, and an all-girl high school on 19 acres. (The elementary portion of the school became co-educational in 1962.) Year after year, graduating seniors enjoy wide acceptance into colleges across the country. I struggle to understand how these students attain high grades while alluring views just outside the windows invite daydreaming on a historic level. Speaking of history, Academy of the Holy Names is Florida's, second-oldest high school.

Academy of Holy Names

I like old schools. Not only did I go to old schools, my wife tells me I am "old school." That's mainly why I'm dragging out these centenarians. They are all in South Tampa and all are testimony to the value this area puts on education. A few years back Wilson Middle School needed new flooring but the budget wouldn't cover installing new wood. Parents, some of whom went there or were the children of parents who had gone there, stepped in and did the carpentry themselves.

I used to try to picture kids doing the same things I was doing, in the same place I was doing it, yet a century earlier. Of course, kids now have a much harder time getting their heads around our pre-device days. Help me out here, has any student passed a real paper note in the last 20 years? Explaining life without texts, Facetime, IM's or hummingbird ringtones, draws blank stares. Tell kids there weren't even beepers when we were back in school and they will ask, "What's a beeper?"

Wilson Midde School - 1915

Mitchell Elementary School - 1915

Back in the day, the desktops we posted our messages on were actual desktops. Using a pen to draw or write on a desk was not permitted but that prohibition was not enforceable, so our school just sanded them clean every summer. Love notes, insults, boasts, scores to settle and simple observations on life were published in these primeval chat rooms daily. With any given room rotating eight periods of 30 or so students, the rumor beast was quickly fed. Desktops also supported prototype video games, but at a pre-microprocessor pace that no modern gamer would be able to tolerate. With eight periods you could have up to eight players but usually just one or two engaged in battle. Player #1 would simply draw a rocket or flying saucer and see how many others wanted in when he returned the next day. Competitors would draw their own spaceships and satellites and show them blasting the original craft with death rays and tracers. From that point it was an interstellar frenzy, one zap or blast at a time. The goal was simply to battle, period by period, day by day, until no space was left.

Ballast Point Elementary School - 1925

Roosevelt Elementary School - 1925

When Henry Plant brought his railroad in 1884 to the fledgling city of Tampa, he continued the line down the nearby peninsula and built a ship terminal at its tip. Port Tampa City grew up around the docks. Tampa and Port Tampa were separate municipalities with miles of scrubland and a hardscrabble community named Rattlesnake between them. The marble-and-glazed tile clad First Bank of Port Tampa opened in 1926. The bank was hit with a double whammy. It failed like so many others in 1929. A federally funded, dredging project diverted much of the shipping to more up-to-date facilities near downtown Tampa. The stately bank building was put to use as a grocery, boutique, a flight school, and health clinic in the decades to come. Port Tampa lingered until it was annexed by Tampa in 1961. Even that would not be a panacea.

My introduction to Port Tampa was as colorful as any of the buildings in this old port community. It was a mission to help my apartment manager find his spouse. He thought she was carrying on with a bartender who worked at one of the Port Tampa watering holes that served nearby MacDill A. F. B. and asked to borrow my car. I didn't know him well enough to give him my keys, and he obviously had been drinking, but I took pity on him. I offered to drive him on the mission. I wasn't shocked by his suspicions because a few days before the wife had shown up at my door in a bathrobe holding a couple of beers. To my relief, we didn't find her.

In 1998, Tampa bought the bank building and converted it into the Port Tampa City Library, which houses a notable collection of nautical artifacts and photos of its old neighborhood.

For the record, I told the wayward wife I was late for a job interview.

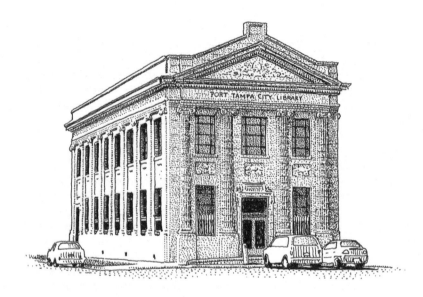

Port Tampa City Library

The West Tampa Branch Library is a pretty unassuming building. Although it is immaculately maintained, the facility looks like a dour uncle among the neighboring exuberant, if somewhat scruffy, buildings. Built in 1914, the library holds the distinction of being the first public library in Hillsborough County. It also is a member of a grand brotherhood of storehouses of knowledge built through the generosity of Scottish-born, industrialist Andrew Carnegie. Between 1883 and 1924 Carnegie funded 2,509 public libraries worldwide, with 1,689 in the United States. In addition to West Tampa and Tampa Heights libraries, Bradenton, Palmetto, Clearwater and St. Petersburg benefitted from Carnegie's philanthropic turn. The West Tampa library stands on land donated by neighborhood cigar magnate Angel Cuesta. Carnegie stipulated that recipients provide the land, the books, and an annual commitment for operations funding.

The Tampa Heights branch has been converted into the county library system's administration center. After college, our daughter Alexandra found herself juggling three part-time jobs, including one at the library. She hoped the job would become full-time and the good news is that when it did she was involved in an outreach and technology program that never required her to "shush" a single patron.

West Tampa Branch Library

The first time I saw the St. James House of Prayer Episcopal Church in Tampa Heights it shouted, "draw me." Eventually, I did. That was before I learned its singular look came from being built from ballast stones fished from the nearby Hillsborough River in 1922. It also was before learning it not only looks like a fort, it was designed by one, Tampa architect Louis A. Fort. It would be a long time before I made the connection between the man who spearheaded the church's construction, the multi-talented Rev. William C. Richardson and my familiar street.

Years earlier, the owner of the house I was renting told me it originally stood on a different lot facing Bayshore Boulevard, half a block away. She also said it was previously owned by Dr. Richardson and the house next door served as lodging for his convalescing patients. I discovered the good doctor, after retiring, had gone to an Episcopal seminary and became Rev. Richardson. At some point, the street he lived on, Dubois Avenue, was renamed Richardson Place. Coming from the Philadelphia area, I nicknamed the house Dilworth Manor, in honor of former Philadelphia mayor Richardson Dilworth. Decades later my neighbors still call it that. At least the Doc/Rev is remembered by his street, even if it is only four blocks long.

St. James House of Prayer Episcopal Church

When we moved to Richardson Place in Hyde Park, our next door neighbors Jim and Celia Ferman had two elementary, school-age daughters. By the time we moved we had watched both daughters walk down the aisle. I made drawings of both daughters' honeymoon homes as presents.
Laura and Preston Farrior's first home has since been replaced with a much larger house so their home only exists in pen and ink. They now live in Laura's grandparents' Hyde Park Bayshore home and I've illustrated that. Janice and Steve Straske briefly lived in Manhattan, NY, and I drew the view from their balcony. This is the first Tampa home for Janice and Steve. Time for another chapter. They would add a second story to this house before they moved. Now, they have three sweet daughters. I have made another gift, a glass dish to celebrate the wedding of their oldest daughter Elly to Adam. Another chapter begins.

3302 W. Mullen Avenue

Jim Cornwell has carved out a successful niche for his State Farm Insurance agency for more than four decades. In his ads he presents his business and himself as stylishly casual. When he commissioned me to illustrate his office I wanted to give it that same vibe. The photo Cornwell uses most often shows him fashionably dressed, his white hair neatly combed, while he relaxes against an implied wall. It is far more compelling than the usual yearbook, redux head-and-shoulder shot. His building fits this feel, its look is contemporary, efficient and unpretentious. For my take I used the view you would get if you were walking up the sidewalk. Full parking bays quietly say there is a lot going on here. I took a lot of reference photographs to find the right angle of approach. My calculations seem to have worked. Not long after I delivered the art, Cornwell asked if I'd be OK with him passing my contact information to fellow agents. He used the image in promotional material and it caught the eyes of several, out-of-state colleagues. I was flattered and all in. The first referral dampened that enthusiasm by sending me blurry Polaroids of a small office jammed into a strip mall in suburban Atlanta. I was able to produce an image that satisfied the customer but it would never find a space in my examples' file.

Jim Cornwell State Farm Insurance

From 1974 Jimmy Mac's was a pioneer of SoHo's (South Howard Avenue) casual dining and drinking scene. Betty and James "Jimmy" McNorrill, Jr., converted an old house into a popular eatery that combined reasonable prices and a convivial atmosphere. At the height of Jimmy Mac's popularity, the McNorrills opened a second location on S. West Shore Boulevard. I took some liberties to make this drawing happen. Jimmy wanted it to reflect a waterfront tone even though the building didn't actually front the water. I climbed onto a nearby trailer to get this perspective and used my pen and ink to bring the bay up to his back door. The restaurant thrived until a developer bought the land under Jimmy's place. Not long after, McNorrill sold the other property and gave Jimmy Mac's a second life in Bryson City, N.C.

Years later, this art would come back to me as an omen. I was creating transfers of my art to fire onto ceramic items. At this stage, I didn't have a reliable source of blank mugs. I remembered seeing lots of mugs at thrift stores so I made the rounds. At a nearby Salvation Army store I didn't turn up any plain white mugs but I did find one with this illustration imprinted on it. Nothing has ever told me to keep on going quite like that mug.

Jimmy Mac's

This house near Bayshore is another rendering that was procured through a school fundraising auction. Although the house isn't far from my own, I didn't know the owners. I do know the owners were happy with the finished art because they wrote a nice thank-you note to show their appreciation.

I almost felt I should send them a thank you. The year before the bid winner tasked me with drawing a tract house absolutely devoid of landscaping, architectural detail, or any character at all. Often, when I am working on a rendering, I take liberties. For the good of the drawing I will remove power lines, street signs and other encumbrances. Dead grass will be revived in pen and ink. Foliage will be pruned to showcase the building behind it. In the case of the naked box I needed to draw, I had to invent lots of greenery just to keep the image from being mistaken for a geometry problem.

Now that our children are grown I no longer offer renderings to be auctioned and no longer live in dread of subjects I may have to breathe life into.

3215 W. Wallcraft Avenue

Up until the late '70s there were numerous, majestic banyan trees scattered around South Tampa. When I drew Bob Baggett's photo studio in 1980, these massive chunks of tree were the only remnants of those mighty banyans. A hard freeze wiped them out. Not long after I did this drawing the tree parts went away. Not much later the vines that I thought made the shop look charming also left. Bigger changes took place inside the shop. Bob's business evolved from film and darkroom into the digital age. Baggett and I frequently compared notes as a couple of old dogs struggled to learn new tricks.

I drove by Bob's place recently and was shocked to discover it had disappeared. We had been out of touch a little longer than I had realized. Naturally, I called to make sure he was OK. He is way better than OK. Someone had come along and offered far more money for his property than he could ever imagine. After 40 years he was ready to move on. Freed from keeping office hours he found that making house calls is highly lucrative. When I got off the phone all I could think was, really, has it been 40 years?

Bob Baggett Photography

Clawd's Crustacean-American Cuisine, like its creator, lived too short a life. In 1994. my good friend Henry Hicks decided to scratch a longtime itch and open a restaurant on Tampa's south Howard Avenue. Henry had a prosperous law practice but multitasking had been second nature to the gregarious attorney. An accomplished cook himself, Hicks knew enough to put one of the area's best chefs in charge. I was honored to help with branding. We zeroed in on the restaurant's signature dish, Maine lobster, and introduced Clawd. Henry was so particular we developed Clawd's own type font, a letter style that fit its look and attitude. Unfortunately, in this case, there were too many owners spoiling the broth. Henry took on business partners with less lofty aspirations. While the restaurant steadily earned stellar reviews from local critics and patrons, the partners focused far more on the bottom line. Impatient for profits, they forced sweeping changes and the place became a sad mishmash of sports bar/saloon. Henry eventually washed his hands of the venture.

That didn't slow my friend down, however. While continuing his law practice he founded a title company, coached middle school basketball, and built a thriving real estate-investment portfolio. He carried on his love of cooking, centered on friends and family. Henry squeezed a lot of living into his life but that life was far too short. Sadly, we lost him to a diving accident on Anna Maria Island at the young age of 60.

Clawds Crustacean-American Cuisine

On Oct. 19, 2002, Tampa residents heard the first clanging of a streetcar bell in more than a half century. The new streetcar system, comprising 10 replica cars, 11 stations and 2.7 miles of track, is a pale shadow of its predecessor. The current line is a single track running from Ybor City to downtown by way of the former Channel District, now Water Street. The downtown transit center for the trolly line was named Dick Greco Plaza Station in 2008. The stations in Ybor City reflect that neighborhood's historic architecture. The 1926 system was a network of tracks that covered 53 miles.

Tampa joined a national post war trend to replace trolleys with buses and cars. The old systems' last car went out of service in 1949. By the time I moved to Tampa almost every trace of the original line had vanished. If you are nostalgia driven, there are remnants to be found. One of the old cars was converted into a cottage in a Sulphur Springs backyard. Volunteers have meticulously restored it and it sits in a Ybor City car barn. The open air station shown here greeted riders at Jules Verne Park in Ballast Point. Ever since the tracks were pulled up, it has served as a park pavilion. Lastly, the broad green parkway, between Bayshore Boulevard's northbound and southbound lanes from Rome Avenue to Gandy Boulevard, was created to provide the streetcars their own right of way. The artifact I'd love to find is Fair Lady, the private streetcar that belonged to Emilia Chapin, owner of the Consumers Electric Light and Street Railroad Company. In the meantime, I console myself with my one, original streetcar token.

Ballast Point Park

Dick Greco Plaza Station

Tampa's Ballast Point is known for two distinctly different reasons. Emilia Chapin developed the park in 1894 as a terminal for the electric trolley line she owned. Jules Verne Park honored the French novelist who selected this spot as the launch site for his popular, futuristic book, "From Earth to Moon." Emilia enhanced the park with a wood pier leading to a pagoda-styled pavilion for gala outings with friends. The neighborhood around the park had long been known as Ballast Point. It was here that the channel leading to Tampa's docks became so shallow that ships were obliged to jettison their ballast stones in order to proceed. Another sort of stone, this one native, is known to geologists around the world as Ballast Point coral. These unusual fossils usually preserve the form of their 30,000-year-old coral polyps on the outside but reveal silky looking strains of chemically replaced agate inside. Long after Emilia departed, the trolley line ended and the pagoda was swept away in a hurricane, the park adopted the name Ballast Point. A newer pier juts 600 feet into Hillsborough Bay and visitors looking for marine and bird life rarely leave disappointed.

I had an interesting meteorological experience there. While fishing on the pier I saw storm clouds forming. They made their predictable, summertime slow march in my direction. Then small flickers of lightning started illuminating those clouds. I heard a faint buzzing coming from a nearby, steel lamp post. Next, little sparks began jumping from my rod's reel to my thumb. The rod's cork handle had served as an insulator and my thumb became a bridge for those charged ions. It was cool seeing small, rapid sparks when my thumb was close and fat, slow sparks as I moved my thumb away. Not wanting to become a human lightning rod, I took a lesson from my thumb and moved myself far from the pier.

Ballast Point Pier

Scottish-born Hugh Campbell MacFarlane reflected on the successful deal he helped broker between the city of Tampa and a consortium of Key West cigar makers, a deal that would create Ybor City, and decided it was time for a sequel. On his own initiative, he purchased 200 acres of vacant land northwest of the little city of Tampa, hoping to duplicate Ybor City's success. To make this work, he had to overcome problems of accessibility and desirability. A primitive flat-bottomed wooden ferry was the only link between MacFarlane's land and the rest of Tampa. Locals had given the area the less than glowing nickname, La Caimanera or Gator Pit. MacFarlane solved that issue with the Fortune Street Bridge which spans the Hillsborough River, connecting West Tampa to Tampa and Ybor City. He also helped incorporate the city of West Tampa in 1895, his successes measured by West Tampa's status in 1912 as Florida's fifth-largest city.

That same year El Centro Espanol's swelling ranks convinced the organization to build a second clubhouse to accommodate West Tampa members. None of the amenities at the other clubs were overlooked at the "El Palacio" as the building was affectionately known. West Tampa would share Ybor City's hardships brought on by the end of the cigar industry's reign and suburban flight. El Palacio had passed into the city of Tampa's hands by the end of the century. After thorough restoration by the city, the building served as a temporary home for the Tampa Museum of Art while its replacement was under construction. During that interval the museum had coffee mugs for sale with this building's image and the Town Tiles logo on the bottom. You didn't think I'd miss a chance to pimp my wares here, did you?

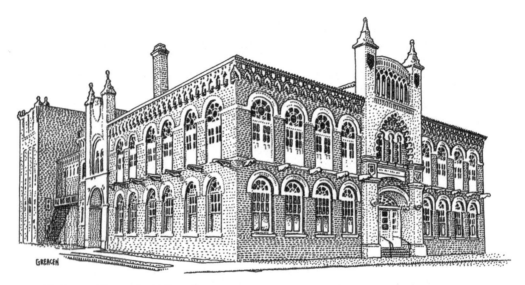

El Centro Espanol of West Tampa

The Sulphur Springs community's colorful history might easily be forgotten without the water tower to serve as a constant reminder. Even with visual cacophony along the route, the tower can't fail to catch the eye of motorists on Interstate 275. Before the electric streetcar line stretched from downtown Tampa to Sulphur Springs, the mineral waters made this a popular bathing resort. Kentucky native Josiah Richardson developed much larger dreams: establishing the Sulphur Springs Hotel and Apartments along with Mave's Arcade. The arcade, which would meet an ignoble end in 1976, was Florida's first shopping mall. To provide potable water for these enterprises, Richardson hired Grover Poole to erect the tower directly over an artesian well on his property. Completed in 1927, the 214-foot tower served Richardson's private water company. When the Depression hit, it ended Richardson's Sulphur Springs dreams, including plans for an elevator to take visitors to the tower's crown. The water company was replaced by the City of Tampa's water system but the tower wasn't about to go away. Poole constructed the tower from poured concrete that employed railroad rails as rebar. The shaft's 45-foot foundation reaches down to bedrock. A grassy park now surrounds it. Of the many bogus tower stories I've heard, my favorite is that it was built as a lookout post to eye pirates coming up the Hillsborough River.

Sulphur Springs Water Tower

It's ironic that the Tampa building that most looks like it could have been designed by Albert Speer wound up being the home of the Bryan Glazer Family JCC. The Fort Homer Hesterly Armory was actually a Washington New Deal project, which explains why it took from 1938 to late 1941 to complete and why no architect has stepped forward to take a bow. From its dedication, the day after the Pearl Harbor attack, to 2001, it was the Tampa headquarters for the Florida Army National Guard and the Army Reserves. The city of Tampa entertained numerous proposals for the property before the Bryan Glazer center opened in 2016. During the Guards' and Reserves' tenure, the cavernous main hall was rented for all kinds of functions. Dr. Martin Luther King, Jr., addressed an audience here as did President John F. Kennedy. JFK's speech at the armory on Nov. 18, 1963 was one of his last. From Tampa, he would make his fateful trip to Dallas. A veritable "who's who" of musicians played in the hall, notably Elvis Presley, James Brown, Pink Floyd, the Allman Brothers, and The Doors. When Mary Denise and I saw Frank Zappa perform he was very much in his element. Perhaps the armory's most enduring association was hosting Championship Wrestling from Florida. The athletic histrionics by the likes of Dusty Rhodes, Andre the Giant, the Brisco Brothers, Mike and Eddie Graham, the Great Malenko, and homeboy Hulk Hogan, drew huge, boisterous crowds. My friend Sonny Esteban shared this childhood experience. Swept up in the crowd's energy, Sonny crumpled up a paper cup and threw it at one of the "bad boy" wrestlers working his way to the ring. Immediately, someone from security clamped his hand on Sonny's shoulder and began dragging him toward expulsion or some other punishment. Suddenly a folding chair, thrown from the balcony, crash landed next to them, setting the cop running after the chair hurler. A good time was had by all.

Fort Homer Hesterly Armory

T.E. Robertson Billiards started out as a pool hall near the University of Tampa in 1930. Twelve years later, Baker's Pool Hall came along and lured away Robertson's customers with a not-so-secret ingredient, air conditioning. By 1950, Robinson had to close his hall but he refused to leave the business he loved. In the spirit of "if you can't beat 'em, join 'em" he opened a pool table, juke box and vending machine service, just across the street from Baker's.

His son Charlie took charge in the '70s and Robertson's went into the pool table manufacturing business. Charlie's son-in-law, Tom Rodgers, hired me to create this exploded view for its sales materials. This was one of those drawings I've wanted an excuse to do for as long as I remember. When I was a kid I would refuse to follow the step-by-step instructions for assembling plastic models. To me that was cheating and I would go by the exploded drawing that gave all the part numbers. Using my method, I always ended up with a few leftover pieces. When I got tired of those models and blew them up with firecrackers (and tell me what red-blooded boy didn't do that?) I could never get them to "explode" like they did in the drawings.

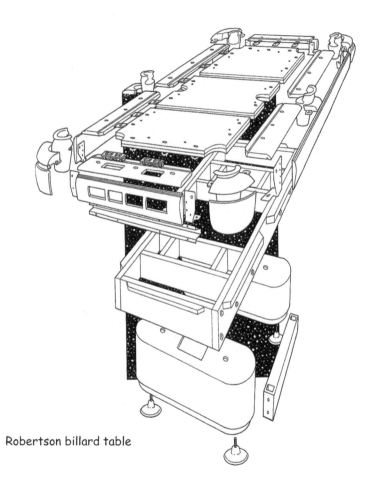
Robertson billard table

EAST OF TAMPA

Cracker Country serves as a reminder that the good old days weren't really that good. The 13 buildings on display at the Florida Fairgrounds, just east of Tampa, give glimpses of life here before air conditioning, indoor plumbing, telephones, or window screens. Founded in 1978, this outdoor museum provides children with valuable lessons about the many skills needed to survive in rustic Florida.

My friend Kristy Andersen rented the grounds when she produced a documentary about African-American author, anthropologist, and filmmaker Zora Neale Hurston. My Model T Ford express wagon and I were hired as extras. Another close friend, Eugenie Bondurant, rode along in my buggy. Eugenie is a professional actor/model with credits in movies, such as "The Conjuring," "Fear of Rain," "The Hunger Games: Mockingjay" (as Tigris) and the cult classic, "Fight Club." My acting career differs, winding up on the cutting-room floor of Kristy's editing studio.

Gretna Church
Early 1900's

Castalia School House
1912

Carlton House
1885

Okahumpka Station
1898

Terry Store
Circa 1890

The Smith House
1894

Governor's Inn
1912

The unincorporated community of Brandon, FL, just east of Tampa, is by all accounts a lovely place to live and work. If there was an award, however, for ugliest main street, Brandon would be a serious contender. Brandon is neither poor nor neglected; to the contrary it is relatively affluent. It doesn't host any noxious industries. Brandon Boulevard, the road the town grew up around, is simply a traffic-choked strip of banality. You can drive this road, State Road 60, from Vero Beach on the Atlantic coast across the state to the gulfClearwater Beach. Your stretch going through Brandon will be punctuated with waits of multiple, traffic-light change cycles at intersection after intersection. You could strain your eyes looking for any roadside architecture of merit.

There is a splendid little oasis in this attenuated desert of dreariness, Stowers Funeral Home. Set respectfully back from the road and shielded from the humdrum by spreading grandfather oaks, stands the former Brandon homestead. James, son of John Brandon, the area's first settler, built it in 1876 and the house has survived with all its Victorian charm. When Dick Stowers bought the home in 1960 to house his funeral business he was fully aware of the historic importance of his acquisition; the business continues to be a diligent custodian. It is sad that you can conduct all manner of business, along the slash of drab, but it takes mourning a loved one to visit this sweet refuge from another time.

Brandon homestead

The sugar cane mill at Dade City's Pioneer Florida Museum and Village demonstrates how sugar was processed between the end of the Civil War and the arrival of modern, mechanical harvesting. The large plantations that relied on enslaved labor were relegated to the dustbin of history. For small landholders, there was a living, a hard one, to be made raising and refining sugar cane. Harvesting was still done using a curved cane knife or a machete. Farming on this reduced scale no longer warranted the large, steam-driven rollers used in pre-war days. Small presses powered by a single horse or mule could get the job done. Similarly, furnaces that boiled sugar into syrup were replaced by smaller, often open air works. Usually, I don't include people in my architectural renderings but in this case Wilbur Dew, a longtime docent at the museum, who died in 2020, seemed to be a necessary component. At the insistence of the museum staff, I revised my drawing to include Wilbur's signature suspenders.

Sugar cane mill

When the C.C. Smith General Store in Lacoochee opened for business it had many of the features today's big box stores boast about. Back in the '20s you could find cashless transactions, a game room, media center, and yes, big boxes. There were a few big differences as well. Business was often transacted without dollar bills because in Lacoochee hardly anyone had any cash. Customers ran a tab and paid if, and when, they could. Gaming took place mostly on a checkerboard. U.S. mail was the media. In the winter, a centrally-placed, potbelly stove turned the general store into a chat room. Most of the store's inventory arrived in barrels, crates and big boxes. Obviously, variety was limited due to its small space. On the plus side, you never had to buy a blister pack of 20 items when you needed just one. Products had to be well made so they would last at least until the final installment was paid.

C.C. Smith's store had a 50-year run, a pretty good span for a mom-and-pop operation. It was restored and replenished in 2000 at the Pioneer Florida Village and Museum in Dade City.

C.C. Smith General Store

Enterprise is a town name brimming with confidence. Sadly, that confidence has not always borne fruit. Florida's first Enterprise grew up on the shore of Lake Monroe after the Second Seminole War in the very unconfidently named Mosquito County, today's Volusia County. After an encouraging start, Enterprise was eclipsed by neighboring towns and finally de-incorporated in 1895. Another community in Pasco County in the late 19th Century aspired to the Enterprise name. This never reached incorporation. Its memory is preserved by an austere gem of a house of worship on the grounds of the Pioneer Florida Museum & Village. Built in 1905, Enterprise United Methodist Church served as a church until 1925. In the early days, the Methodist community depended on a circuit-riding reverend to hold once-a-month services. The sanctuary was brought to the museum grounds in 1977. Despite its Spartan interior, or just maybe because it is, the chapel is now a thriving venue for weddings.

Enterprise United Methodist Church

Florida Southern College's President Ludd Spivey knew what he wanted and how to get it. If the little Lakeland college founded in 1883 was ever going to be more than a minor, regional institution it needed something to set itself apart. Spivey invited the era's best-known architect to develop a master plan for the campus. That was the "what he wanted" part. The "how to get it" was letting architect Frank Lloyd Wright have absolutely free hand in the project.

The Annie Pfeiffer Chapel, Wright's first building completed in 1941, proved the wisdom of Spivey's arrangement. Florida Southern has adopted the bowtie design, students call it God's bicycle rack, on the chapel's 65-foot tower as an icon for the school. Between 1941 and 1958, Wright had a green light to continue designing. The school became the largest grouping of FLW buildings anywhere. Just as the architect paid as much attention to interior design as he did to exterior design, Wright felt compelled to address the space between the college buildings. For this compact campus to be ideally walkable he tied various units together with esplanades, or covered walkways, to shelter pedestrians from scorching sun and unpredictable rain. These low overhangs are a signature Wright touch. He had a tendency to scale his designs around his own not-so-lofty height.

Annie Pfeiffer Chapel

When I asked my college buddy, Jader, to be part of my marriage to Mary Denise Scourtes, his first words were, "Does that mean you're going to have to dive for the cross?" That is how pervasive the Tarpon Springs Epiphany celebration has become. For the record, my wife is Tampa born and bred, but her Greek-American family has wonderful relatives in Tarpon.

In the 1880s, this relatively quiet, gulf-side town began attracting spongers from the Bahama Islands and Key West. They could make a modest living using poles with hooked tips to retrieve sponges from the shallow estuaries. By 1905, John Cocoris introduced Greek-style sponging and the business flourished. Helmeted divers harvested larger catches by going into deeper water. Immigrant divers from the Aegean Islands helped make Tarpon the city in the U.S. with the largest Greek-American population. More than one in 10 residents claims Greek descent. Sponging operates mostly as a novelty for the tourist industry. Tarpon's railroad station dates back to 1909, making it one of the area's oldest. The Tarpon Springs Historical Train Depot now stores memories as the home of the Tarpon Springs Area Historical Museum. The right-of-way where trains once ran now, is part of the county-long Fred Marquis Pinellas Trail for walking, jogging and biking.

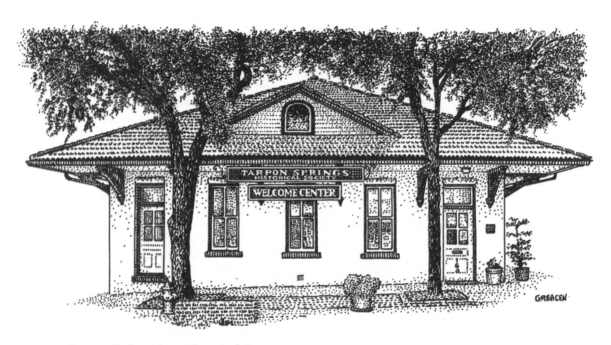

Tarpon Springs Area Historical Museum

As the oldest surviving home in Florida's Pinellas County, the McMullen-Coachman Log Cabin has my respect. Its story has made me more fond of this treasure. At 18, James McMullen became ill with what in the mid-19th Century was called consumption, AKA tuberculosis. The treatment prescribed was to pack some clothes and a bed roll and walk himself from his family home in Georgia to Central Florida. Not only did the cure work but soon after he planned to relocate to the eden that provided his salvation. Not all was bliss in his new wilderness home, however.

When hostilities broke out with the Seminoles, he and his bride were forced to abandon their newly built cabin, only to find it burned when they returned. His second cabin, completed in 1852, is the one that holds the "oldest" title for Pinellas County. In 1977, the cabin was donated to the city of Largo and moved to Heritage Village, a collection of pioneering Pinellas structures.

Part of McMullen's cure was getting as much fresh air as possible so he built his Florida cabin with "enough space between the logs to throw a cat through." Never mind the flies, mosquitoes, snakes and other vermin this would allow. Who goes around throwing cats between logs? There is nothing in McMullen's account about bringing pets along on his self exile so hopefully no felines were harmed in the making of this analogy.

McMullen-Coachman Log Cabin

The drive along Pinellas Park's Park Boulevard presents an almost unbroken string of glass, neon and plastic. There remains a notable exception, Park Feed Store, next to the railroad crossing at 58th Street. Its building dates back before there was a Pinellas Park. Built in 1892, the structure was moved to its current site in 1915 where it would serve as a bakery for 17 years. For the decade following the place would be home to curiously checkered occupants including a general store, beer hall, a church and a house of ill repute. Finally, the building entered its longest lasting gig as a feed store in 1942. Since the time the building arrived at its present location one aspect has remained consistent, ownership by the Ponath family, now in its third generation. The post war years saw Pinellas Park transition from agricultural to residential and Park Feed has been savvy enough to evolve with the trend. Brad Gentile and his brother Adam shepherded the Pinellas Park store and another historic one in Largo into the non-farm era. The old shop, like the official store cat, Smokey, seems to have nine lives.

Park Feed Store

"If you believe that, I have swampland in Florida to sell you" is the popular expression. In the early 1900s, many colorful characters made, and often lost, fortunes doing just that. C. Perry Snell was an example; the Kentucky druggist moved to St. Petersburg in 1900 and caught the developer/speculator bug. Bethia Coffey, writing in the St. Petersburg Evening Independent, referred to Snell as half con man. (The Independent had its own promotional hustle, offering free copies if the sun failed to come out the previous day.) In October, 1925, Perry's masterpiece went on the marketplace, touted with epithets, such as "laughing waters amid flowers in bloom" and "domes and towers hold sway." Never mind that at the time only 39 of Snell Isle's 275 acres were above the high tide line. Snell built his own luxurious home there in 1928. In 2009, the freshly remodeled mansion was listed for sale at $18 million. Snell, who was married four times, died broke in 1942.

Syndicated cartoonist Wally Bishop, another St. Petersburg notable, lived in the Snell House in the mid '90s. Wally and his wife Louise were active supporters of the local arts scene. From 1927 to 1974 Wally penned a daily comic strip "Mugs and Skeeter." In the opinion of another cartoonist (me), his work was endearing, but not particularly funny.

Perry Snell House

The front facade of St. Petersburg's Museum of Fine Arts looks like a museum that aspired to the big leagues. The back side gives the look of one that has already gotten there. Although the MFA's neoclassical portico has a "been there forever" look, the building opened in 1965. When expansion in 2008 doubled the museum's size, Bay area architect Yann Weymouth set aside the traditional and opted for openness and light.

While not on the scale of counterparts in some of our major cities, the museum has a large, enviable collection. European masters such as Monet, Rodin and Corot are represented. So are American artists George Inness, Andrew Wyeth, George Bellows and Georgia O'Keeffe. Ancient art, art glass and photographs round out the collection. The MFA enjoys the virtue of accessibility. I grew up in awe of the Philadelphia Museum of Art and its renowned collection. Somehow, though, housed in its Greco-Roman temple perched atop its own acropolis overlooking the Philly skyline, it always seemed aloof. Sandwiched between Old Tampa Bay and the trendy cafes along Beach Drive, the MFA seems to beckon you inside to taste a little art.

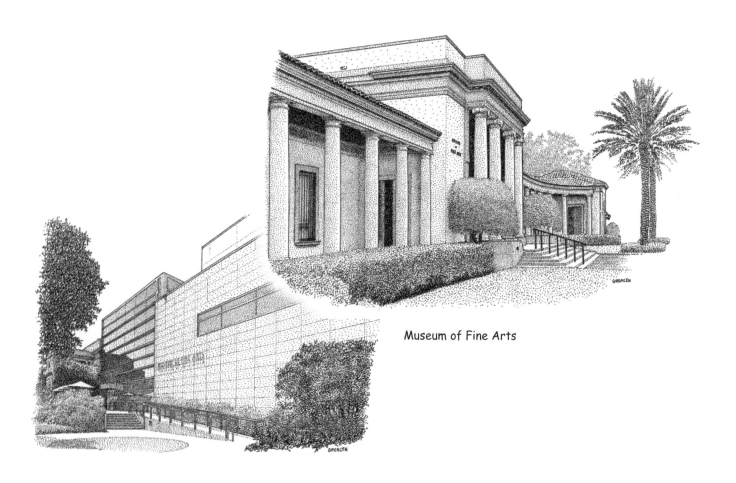

Museum of Fine Arts

Downtown St. Petersburg has a number of museums, among them the Museum of Fine Arts, The Dali and the James Museum of Western & Wildlife Art, which celebrate the creativity of mankind. Then there is one with a grim but just as necessary mission, The Florida Holocaust Museum. This museum was founded in 1992 and in 1998 moved into its present, purpose-built location. The museum's facade, designed by Israeli-born Nick Benjacob successfully signals somber without resorting to maudlin. Exhibits are arranged to show the banal ways intolerance can seep into everyday life if left unchecked, ultimately taking on grotesque proportions.

The museum's centerpiece, one of the many, many boxcars employed by the Final Solution simply goes by its railcar designation #113 069-5. The disconnect seems astonishing. Here was a highly educated nation of people that took the time to track every man, woman and child, sent through the hellish maze of concentration and death camps and not a voice condemning this horror was heard. The lasting imperative of the museum is not only to remind us of past evils of intolerance but to warn us of their threat today and tomorrow.

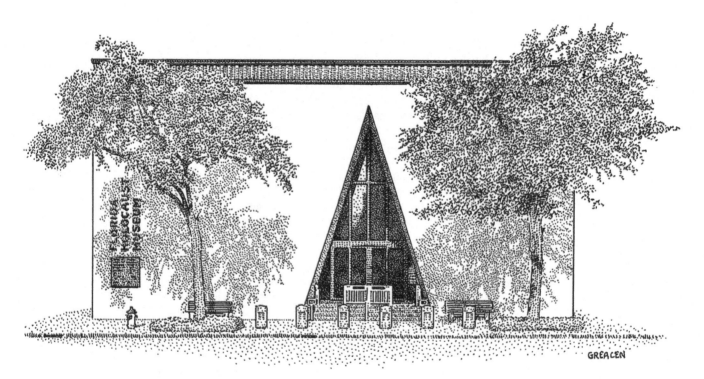

The Florida Holocaust Museum

St. Petersburg was considered the sleepy neighbor across the Bay when I moved to Tampa in the early '70s. It was a quaint throwback where you could find a parking space downtown, even at noon. St. Pete's aging population earned it the nickname "Heaven's Waiting Room." Downtown was best known for its green benches and the senior citizens flocking to them. Tampans thought of themselves as the young, cool kids. Sometime after the new millennium, St. Pete caught Tampa napping and captured the cool. A vibrant arts scene blossomed seemingly overnight. Big events came to town. The annual Grand Prix of St. Petersburg took over the streets. Cookoffs and music festivals packed the waterfront. No single building better heralds St. Pete's transition to hip than the museum housing the world's largest collection of Salvador Dali's work known as The Dali. Opened in January, 2011, it houses the largest and most significant body of the artist's work outside Europe. Architect Yann Weymouth's (chief of design for I.M. Pei Paris' Grand Louvre project) depiction is mold breaking in a way Salvador would approve. The glass-segmented skylight, called "Enigma," harkens to Dali's deft unpredictability.

Just as Dali's surrealist masterpiece "The Persistence of Memory," is his most-recognized painting, Weymouth turned illumination into imagination. With Tampa's completion of a six-mile-plus Riverwalk, connecting multiple museums and entertainment venues, the city has some serious catching up to do. Hopefully, this healthy competition has a long future.

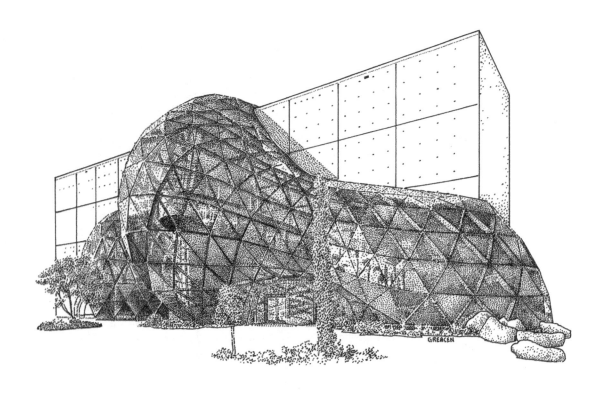

The Dali

I miss St. Petersburg's inverted pyramid pier. Even detractors had to admit the pier was unique, which says a lot as there have been many piers on the waterfront. After making its way to St. Petersburg in 1889, the Orange Belt Railroad extended its tracks 2,000 feet over the bay on Railroad Pier. Although built for the purpose of transferring cargo to ships, the railroad recognized its entertainment value and added a bathing pavilion. Other strictly pleasure-oriented piers would soon spring up. The Brantley Pier, Electric Pier, Municipal Pier, and the Fountain of Youth Pier AKA the Tomlinson Pier, drew crowds. After the Tampa Bay Hurricane of 1921, only the Railroad Pier remained. In 1926, the city of St. Petersburg filled the void with a Mediterranean-revival palace called Million Dollar Pier, which featured a grand ballroom, the WSUN-AM 590 broadcast studio and streetcar service. It enjoyed a 40-year run. The inverted pyramid opened in 1973, the same year I arrived in Tampa. I was awed by this giant iron lotus. For years, a meticulously reconstructed version of the HMS Bounty, used in the MGM movie "The Mutiny of the Bounty," called The Pier its home port. (It tragically went down in 2013 with its captain off North Carolina during Hurricane Sandy.) Soon after, the city issued the pyramid's death sentence, an open-and-shut case of unstable pilings was called the crime. The St. Pete Pier, which opened in 2020, and 26-acre Pier District, will provide generations a way to enjoy Tampa Bay. I like to dream of an episode of the television show "Antiques Roadshow," far into the future, with an appraiser ooh-ing and aah-ing over a proud heirloom, one of my imprinted, inverted-pyramid pier mugs.

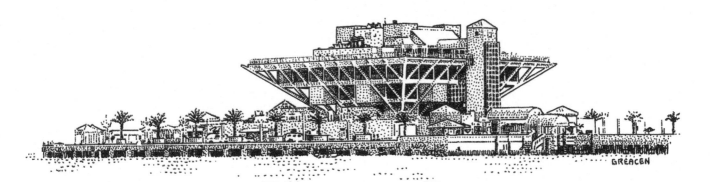

St. Petersburg Pier

SOUTH FLORIDA

The freighter Summit Venture was caught in a sudden squall and rammed the original Skyway Bridge on May 9, 1980, taking out the southbound span. Thirty-five people died in the tragic event when several cars, a pick-up truck and a Greyhound bus plunged into Tampa Bay. The bridge that would replace both spans in 1987 has become a symbol for the area thanks to its elegant, forward-looking design. Years later, I was reminded of that squall (meteorologists called it a microburst), while Mary Denise and I were waiting at the Miami airport for a delayed flight from London. A fellow traveler regaled us with tales of near brushes with disaster, each account more harrowing than the last. At a pause I said I'd never experienced anything of the sort but his stories reminded me of the man on that fateful morning whose car stopped a mere 14 inches from the edge of the missing span of the Skyway. Unwittingly, I had baited a trap he could not resist. Without hesitation, he jumped in with how the storm causing the accident had forced him to spend the previous night in a motel and how he was a heartbeat from mayhem. Except there wasn't a storm the night before. The harbor pilot who was initially blamed would be exonerated by the instantaneous nature of the storm. When my wife returned from searching for an alternative flight, our danger ranger had ratcheted up to more incredible tales. These seemed compelling to Mary Denise until I eased behind the guy and gave her the internationally recognized "cuckoo" sign.

Sunshine Skyway Bridge

The Wiggins Store serves as the administrative office, museum shop and exhibit space for Manatee Village, an assemblage of rescued historic buildings in Bradenton, FL. Wiggins is the only structure still on its original site. It's a fairly unassuming brick building with an inviting, wrap-around porch. In its day, King Wiggins' store was the commercial heart of the long-gone town of Manatee. Everything from dry goods to Victor Bicycles could be found in this mercantile outpost. Wiggins even offered hotel rooms to accommodate far flung customers. In 1903, when the store was built, modern air conditioning was not part of the equation. Broad-covered porches, deep, double-hung windows and insulation, air pockets built into the brick walls were the technology at hand to deal with summer's sweltering heat. Many of the hearty pioneers who endured the primitive conditions lie in the Old Manatee Burial Ground next to the park.

Wiggins Store

Old Cabbage Head is the endearing, if not flattering, name of the steam locomotive on the grounds of Bradenton's Manatee Village Historical Park. Built by Philadelphia's Baldwin Locomotive Works in 1913, the engine served North Florida turpentine production camps before coming to the Bradenton area in 1948. There it put in just six years for the Nocatee-Manatee Crate Company before it was relegated to the scrap yard. Fortunately, the Manatee County Historical Society made the wise decision to buy and preserve the old engine.

Its cabbage name comes from the unusual, bulbous shape of the engine's smokestack. Wide, flaring smokestacks were a feature more common on earlier, wood-burning engines. Burning wood for fuel emitted hazardous burning embers in its exhaust. Wide screens were placed over an engine's stack to prevent the residue from starting fires in a train's wake. Although Old Cabbage was built to be a coal burner to reduce the risk, her service in the fire-prone piney woods called for extra precaution. Although coal proved a safer fuel, it was dirtier and it blackened everything it came in contact with. That is why the brightly painted locomotives with their shiny brass fittings had given way to basic black when Old Cabbage Head came along.

Old Cabbage Head

If Anna Maria City Pier ever adopts a mascot, it should be the phoenix. It has risen from the ashes, or more accurately the waves, time and time again. City Pier was built in 1911 as a dock for steamers carrying the island's first vacationers. Within a decade the first bridge would open the island to cars and the transportation value of the pier would rapidly fade away. That would not put a dent in the pier's popularity. A small restaurant, a bait shop, 600 feet of fishing dock and a glorious view of the mouth of Tampa Bay, has drawn a steady stream of visitors. The only thing that could dent the old attraction is hurricanes and many of them have. City Pier was roughed up a few times in the mid '70s and took additional blows in 1988 and 2012. Irma spared most of the Bay area but singled out the pier for serious punishment. This time the damage was nearly total and its recovery slow. Steel beams have replaced wood ones and it will take a while for the Gulf's salty water to paint a warm patina on the new amenities. The radiant sky above and the blue water below are as grand as ever. The pier lives on.

Anna Maria City Pier

The Anna Maria City Jail was built almost as a joke. Big time crime was not an issue in the early days, but local "troublemakers," often young men who had quaffed a few too many, became a frequent annoyance. The city addressed the problem with this single cellblock in 1927. Public humiliation was the intended consequence but a lack of screens let mosquitoes dole out additional punishment. Fire consumed the jail's wooden components in 1940, leaving the hollow shell as a colorful, tourist posing site. What I love about the building is its tabby, the material that it is made of.

Feline fanciers need not worry. Tabby is a primitive form of cement, composed of sand, water and broken sea shells that could be formed like building blocks or more frequently poured into ceiling level forms to create walls, floors and foundations. It was introduced into Florida by the earliest Spanish settlers and has a long history in Anna Maria's neighboring towns. The Braden Castle (now in ruins) and the lovingly restored Gamble Mansion are notable antebellum examples of local tabby usage.

Anna Maria City Jail

The U.S. Congress published an exhaustive study commemorating the 400th anniversary of the Hernando de Soto expedition in 1939. The trail had gone cold and the eyewitness accounts left a lot to be desired geographically. The official report gave Bradenton, FL, the dubious honor of the disembarkment site. Our National Park Service built and maintains an interpretive reproduction of the landing camp and native neighborhood. It's an enjoyable visit as long as you block out the mayhem that the expedition unleashed and don't mind that this spot most likely is not the real location. Since that report was published, archeological spade work and intriguing studies of the event preserved in Native American oral traditions have given historians a lot more information. Further south, Port Charlotte most likely is the invasion site. Until this juggernaut arrived, the Caloosas to the south and the Timucuans to the north claimed ownership of the land. Hernando germs were far more powerful than his cannons. When refugees from Georgia and Alabama started rebranding themselves as Seminoles in Florida, they entered a vacuum, but it didn't last. That land grab known as "Manifest Destiny" would squeeze the Seminoles down to the least-inviting portion of Florida swamp land. There the hearty survivors resorted to living in chickees, log and palm frond-homes like the reproduction at the De Soto National Memorial. Perhaps chickees were inherited from the earlier tribes. More evidence probably remains underground.

Chickee

After the Second Seminole War wound down in 1842, homesteaders were drawn to peninsular Florida with dreams of setting up a plantation system similar to those in older, Southern states. The Greek-revival mansion Robert Gamble built between 1845 and 1850 signaled his grand aspirations. Few other homes built at the time displayed such opulence; no others survived. Gamble's personal fortune did not fare as well; he would lose both the house and the land to creditors before the Civil War broke out. After the war the sleepy little town of Ellenton formed around the estate. The mansion proved too costly to be kept as a residence and early in the 20th Century at its nadir served as a fertilizer warehouse. In 1920, the United Daughters of the Confederacy spearheaded efforts to preserve this relic. In its restored condition it is a virtual window into life in antebellum Florida.

When I read about the site I invited my friend John Whitehead to take the 40-mile trip from Tampa to visit. He wanted to bring along his grandmother, "Granny." Kate Whitehead had arrived in Ellenton by steamboat in 1906 along with her family. She spent her youth in Ellenton before moving to Tampa in 1944. It had been years since her last return. Her most touching recollection was at the mansion. On the second floor veranda she received her first kiss from the man who would become John's grandfather.

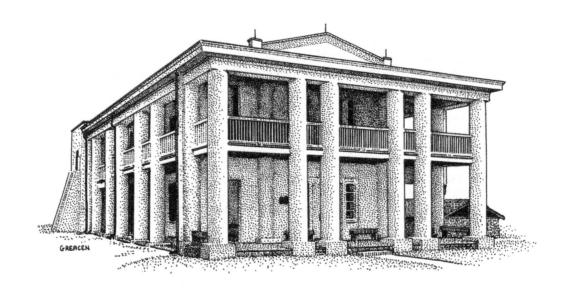

Gamble Mansion

Sarasota's Ca' d'Zan, Venetian for House of John, embodies the exotic tastes and opulent lifestyle of circus impresario John Ringling. Having established the winter quarters for the "Greatest Show on Earth," in this sleepy, gulfside town, John and Mabel Ringling built their flamboyant, Venetian Gothic revival mansion at the edge of Sarasota Bay. Costing $1.5 million, it was completed in 1926. Ringling would die a decade later, the last siblings of the founding Ringling family. Besides his showpiece home, his legacy lives on with the extensive art collection in Sarasota's Ringling Museum. In 1967, descendants sold the Ringling Brothers, Barnum and Bailey Circus to another set of brothers, Irwin and Israel Feld. In 1971, they sold the circus to Mattel, then purchased it back from the toy company in 1981. Feld Entertainment in Ellenton, FL, folded Ringling's tent in 2017. In 2021, the family generated rumors of restarting the circus yet again.

Another remnant from the circus' Florida presence is Showtown, AKA Gibsontown, a little way up Highway 41 from Sarasota. Circuses had, believe it or not, their own caste system and "Gib-Town" became home to the sideshow people and carnival workers. Giant's Camp Lodge and Fish Camp, opened by Aurelio "Al" Tomaini the "World's Tallest Man," is gone and the exterior art on the Showtown Bar & Grill isn't up to its old standards but the prevalence of hand-painted signs and portable rides parked in resident's yards remind you that the show must go on.

Ca' d'Zan at the John and Mable Ringling Museum of Art

Thomas and Mina Edison weren't simply snowbirds when they moved to Fort Myers, FL, in 1885. The always curious Tom went there to do some prospecting. Whereas most visitors at the time viewed the nearly impenetrable, subtropical growth surrounding them as exotic, but valueless, Edison saw it as a gold mine of raw materials. Not content to live in just any house, he drew plans and had his "Seminole Lodge" prefabricated in Maine then shipped to its destination on the banks of the 67-mile Caloosahatchee River, named for the Calusa tribe. The house was connected by breezeway to the home of a trusted, business partner. When that partner made a decision that Edison disapproved of, Tom cut off the utilities to the neighbor's residence.

Fortunately, Edison's relationship with next door friend Henry Ford, yes, that Ford, fared better. Just outside the Edison/Ford complex's museum and shop there is a living monument to the "Wizard of Menlo Park." In 1925, he planted a 4-foot ficus tree, which today has grown into a towering, one-acre-diameter, banyan tree. It is just one of roughly 1,000 varieties of plants he amassed on his gorgeous, Florida property.

Edison Winter Home

Two of our pre-eminent, entrepreneur inventors, Thomas Edison and Henry Ford, once employer and employee, remained lifelong friends. The camping vacations they took, along with tire magnate Harvey Firestone and naturalist Edgar Rice Burroughs, were celebrity events. Henry and Clara Ford enjoyed visiting the Edisons at their Fort Myers winter home so much they bought "the Mangoes," a bungalow-style house next door. Just like Edison, Ford soon set up a workshop so he could continue tinkering while on vacation. Ford famously gifted his neighbor with a Model T Ford, which was custom equipped with extra-wide axles. These allowed Edison to follow logging wagon paths, which often were the only way to gain access, into the thick jungle surroundings.

Ford and Edison shared many genius traits, yet each was enormously stubborn, which sometimes worked to their detriment. Edison publicly feuded with industrialist George Westinghouse and inventor Nikola Tesla over which technology would serve as the foundation of the electric grid used today. Edison championed direct current (DC) systems and the later alternating current (AC). Edison was reluctant to give up cylinder recordings when the rest of the industry went to discs. After he capitulated, his discs were made to revolve at a different speed and he continued to market his cylinder-recorded machines as an office-dictation device. After a $15 million car production run, Ford reluctantly gave in to public demand for a more modern design than the Model T, only after his company lost its dominance of the market.

Ford Winter Home

Miami's historic preservation community was given a huge gift from television producer Michael Mann when he made the city's Art Deco district a backdrop for his sun-splashed, crime series, "Miami Vice." The national attention helped efforts to preserve this square-mile home to some 900 significant structures. The Cardozo Hotel, built in 1939, designed by architect Henry Huhauser and currently owned by singers Gloria Estefan and her husband Emilio Estefan, is featured in "There's Something About Mary" and "Any Given Sunday." It's on the National Register of Historic Places and will be around long after people have forgotten fictional Miami detectives Crocket and Tubbs.

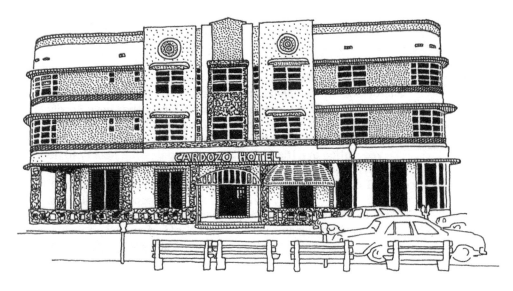
Cardozo Hotel

Pigeon Key looks like a mere speck when viewed from the Seven Mile Bridge, which connects Knights Key to Little Duck Key. On it is a cluster of modest, worker dormitories that have hardly changed since the days when Henry Flagler pushed his oversea railroad down to Key West. Occasional hurricanes scrub the vegetation off the pint-sized outcrop but the hearty little buildings have endured and now house a marine-biology learning center. I bunked here a couple of nights on a trip years ago with my son's St. John's Episcopal School class.

The accommodations, to put it mildly, were rustic, and led me to cross "bridge maintenance worker" off of my list of viable, alternative vocations.

Pigeon Key railroad workers' dormitory

Key West's James Audubon House has the distinction of being one of the places the namesake painter and printmaker did not stay during his time there. Invoking the artist's name was, in part, a ploy Mitchell and Frances Wolfson used to prevent this early Key West home from being replaced by a parking lot. The house, built by Captain Geiger, Key West's first harbor pilot in the early 1800s, captures the feel of those years and houses an impressive collection of the naturalist's work. Foliage from the Geiger property did make its way into some of Audubon's prints. The grounds are an inspiration for serious gardeners. Also, there is not a single T-shirt shop within line of sight.

The Audubon House

The Ernest Hemingway Home and Museum in Key West is many things to many people. For aspiring writers, it is an opportunity to reverse engineer Hemingway's literary success by observing the site where much of his work took place. For vacationing college students it's something, other than drinking all night and puking up and down Duval Street, to tell their parents about. And of course, for crazy cat ladies and other feline fanciers, it is nirvana. Hemingway named all of his cats after famous people. Some of the 60 cats here are descendants of his original, chawky, six-towed, Snow White.

Cats rule here, slumbering everywhere, and seemingly ask for attention despite the "please do not touch" signs.

Ernest Hemingway Home and Museum

Lighthouses normally are situated on rocky islands or jutting points of shoreline. Normal doesn't apply in the Conch Republic where The Key West Lighthouse is in the center of a town. The rationale? The island lost a waterfront light to a hurricane and the folks weren't going to make that mistake twice. This replacement was first lit in 1848. Even though the lighthouse location was about 15 feet above sea level, the 50-foot tower couldn't be seen from far away. An upgrade came in 1873 when it received a new lamp and the building was raised an additional 3 feet. In 1894, the lighthouse's shaft was extended another 20 feet. The navigational aid was decommissioned in 1969.

No longer an aid to navigators, the landmark has been leased to the Key West Museum of Art & History at the Custom House ever since. The beacon provides a great bird's eye view of this exotic village.

Key West Lighthouse

NORTH FLORIDA

Sugar was a harsh, labor-intensive industry until mechanization arrived in the middle of the last century. Christopher Columbus is credited with introducing the crop to the Western Hemisphere when sugar harvesting rapidly spread throughout the Caribbean Basin and beyond. European planters thought they would have a cheap, abundant labor source in the native population but brutal working conditions, coupled with foreign germs, quickly wiped out the majority of the original inhabitants. Plantation owners turned to importing enslaved Africans who were less susceptible to Old World diseases.

David Levi Yulee is best known in Florida for creating the state's first major railroad system. He also is notable for representing the state as the first Jewish U.S. senator. His fortune came from his 5,000-acre Yulee Sugar Mill and the 1,000 slaves that bore the brunt of the brutal work.

The succession he stridently championed would idle his railroad. Burned by federal raiders, his sugar business never recovered. Just as the Second Seminole War spelled the end of sugar planting on Florida's Atlantic coast, the Civil War brought the demise of sugar as a major industry on the state's Gulf coast. All that remains today are a few brooding ruins such as the ones here at Homosassa.

Yulee Sugar Mill Ruins State Park

Just north of Ocala, U.S. Route 441 verges off U.S. Route 301, the pre-interstate artery serving points north. U.S. 301 continues through a string of formerly notorious speed-trap towns such as Waldo, Lawtey and Starke.

Route 441 leads you into Gainesville, home of the University of Florida. Along the latter piece of road, there are towns that have, for better or worse, kept time at bay. If you stick to the highway your impression of McIntosh will be formed by a rambling, old, packing house, a quaint country church and a small cluster of nondescript buildings. If you head east into town, you enter a tunnel of spreading oaks, Spanish moss and houses that were built for front porch living. Streets end at the shore of Lake Orange.

When the railroad was pulled up the town wisely saved the old station, which now serves as a museum. When I illustrated it, huge live oaks, large enough for Keebler elves, shaded the quaint Merrily Bed & Breakfast, which was built in 1888.

This drawing was one of my series of illustrations for the award-winning, "Guide to the Small and Historic Lodgings of Florida," by Herb Hiller (Pineapple Press). Hiller spent most of his career in the travel industry. With this book he changed gears figuratively and literally. Instead of flying around the state creating content for glossy publications, he criss-crossed by bicycle to write engaging descriptions of the many hotels and lodgings he examined. Herb found a small publishing house to print his work and pitched it in pure Florida huster form. Mary Denise and I had the pleasure of hosting him for a Hyde Park overnight stay when he cycled here on a statewide interview circuit.

Merrily Bed & Breakfast

Micanopy, FL, made its national debut in 1991 as the setting for fictional Grady, SC, in the romantic comedy, "Doc Hollywood." Sister town McIntosh, just down the road supplied some backdrop, too. The appeal of this little town is its appearance of having been suspended in time. It's not just the old buildings and overarching oaks, it is the prevailing languid pace of the place. Seminole chiefs, an army outpost and fruit shippers have come and gone but the town of Micanopy gets by, by just getting by. Bed & breakfasts and antique stores are the town's most recent sustaining force. The old packing house, once the motor that ran the town, is an appropriate repository for the Micanopy Historical Society Museum. Visitors find an abundance of local artifacts and pride of place. One major player in corporate America totally gets it. One wall of the packing house-turned-museum bears a vintage Coke advertisement painted on the old wood siding. Coca-Cola corporate representatives keep tabs on the sign and provide retouching when weathering makes it necessary.

Micanopy Historical Society Museum

Kanapaha, the Historic Haile Homestead on the outskirts of Gainesville, is not the kind of plantation house brought to mind by "Gone With the Wind." What it lacks in ostentation though, it makes up for in rock-solid construction. Heart of pine beams held together by mortise and tenon joinery and cypress siding enabled the home to survive decades of standing empty. Thomas and Esther Haile built the home in 1856 after moving there from Camden, SC. Originally, they came to raise sea island cotton but after that market collapsed they farmed fruits and vegetables.

The uncomplicated exterior gives no clue to the surprise that awaits visitors inside. Interior walls are embellished with handwritten words, approximately 12,500 of them, called "The Talking Walls." Some of the writing dates back to the 1850s. It almost makes my son's University of Florida fraternity room (SAE) and apartment, look tame by comparison. Almost.

Historic Haile Homestead

Sometimes mistaken as Florida's bat tower located elsewhere on campus, this is the Century Tower, a belfry sporting 61 bells. The University of Florida's original campus design called for a gothic tower placed at its center. It took three years for Century Tower to be completed. Even then, it had to rely on fake, recorded bells for another 19 years before a full carillon was installed. The 61 chimes that make up this instrument range from a modest 15-pounder to B-flat gong that weighs a whopping 7,000 pounds. Playing the bells, according to UF alum Wade Fitzgerald, a musician who enjoyed the experience, requires the wingspan of an albatross and the legs of a giraffe. Some serious endurance is a help too, as the 12-story edifice has no elevator. The tower was intended to be the university's signature landmark but every Gator knows that title belongs to The Swamp, AKA Steve Spurrier-Florida Field at Ben Hill Griffin Stadium,

At one time, Century Tower had its own swamp, a man-made moat intended for raising mascot alligators. As one might guess, that wasn't as good an idea as it originally sounded. No trace of that moat is there today. If you want to see gators, hit The Swamp.

Century Tower

Apalachee Parkway, the stretch of Florida Highway 27 leading into Tallahassee, FL, leads you up a broad incline to the front steps of the historic, old Capitol. It makes an impressive greeting. No longer used for the day-to-day business of government, it benignly masks the new Capitol that replaced it. Besides a general lack of charm, the Florida State Capitol exhibits a singular phallic profile. Mostly ceremonial events take place today in the old building, its core dating back to 1845. Recent restoration has taken it back to the way it appeared in 1906.

Tallahassee takes pride in having been the only state capital east of the Mississippi not taken by federal forces before the end of the Civil War. In reality, this is due less to any valiant defense than a lack of strategic value. Prior to joining the United States, Florida was administered as halves, the east governed from St. Augustine, and the west from Pensacola. Tallahassee was a compromise between those entities and some critics contend it has remained compromised ever since.

The Florida State Capitol

Fort Matanzas' name is derived from the Spanish word for "slaughter," which comes from a grim event, massacre at Matanzas Inlet, dating centuries before the picturesque, little outpost was completed in 1742. The fort's cannons only fired on an enemy once and a single round was enough to repulse a flotilla of rampaging, British-backed Georgians. Built of the same soft coquina stone as its bigger brother, the Castillo San Marcos in St. Augustine is a lonely fortification protecting the southern approach to the city. By the time the Spanish left Florida it sat abandoned on uninvitingly named Rattlesnake Island. In 1916, on the brink of collapse, the relic was stabilized and restored by the Department of Defense and in 1933 turned over to the National Park Service.

Fort Matanzas National Monument

St. Augustine is a wonderful city, teeming with old world charm, but sometimes it takes its own hype too seriously. No, Ponce DeLeon's rejuvenating spring is not here. "America's oldest city" is in reality the oldest, continuing European settlement in the continental United States. Pedro Menendez de Aviles first established a toehold on Anastasia Island in 1565 (40 years after San Juan, Puerto Rico, came into being). The colony started where St. Augustine now stands after a hurricane wiped out the original settlement. The Gonzalez-Alvarez House makes a claim to being America's oldest house. Archeologists have confirmed there was a structure built in the 1600s at this location. Gonzalez-Alvarez House, however, only dates back to 1723. That reduces the "oldest house" bragging rights to within Florida's borders. That date only applies to the coquina stone first floor. The wood-built second story was added during the city's British period, after 1763. This National Historic Landmark, at 14 Saint Francis St., is a charming venue, lovingly maintained since 1918 by the St. Augustine Historical Society and well worth the visit.

Gonzalez-Alvarez House

About the Author

Charles Greacen was born in Camden, NJ, and was raised in the nearby town of Merchantville. He attended Denison University in Granville, OH, earning his Bachelor of Fine Arts degree and receiving fellowships in both the school's Fine Arts and Classics departments.

After graduating, he moved to Tampa, FL, and embarked on a career in the graphic arts field. He worked at the Tampa Tribune and Tampa Times as a staff artist, then Brewmasters Steakhouse, Inc. as Advertising and Public Relations Manager before opening his art studio, Charles Greacen Illustration & Graphics. Over the years CGI&G created logos, maps, cartoons and illustrations for all forms of print media. He produced a cartoon for two years for The Tampa Tribune and for 17 years published a weekly, topical cartoon for the Tampa Bay Times (formerly named St. Petersburg Times).

Almost 15 years ago he merged his rendering skills with an urge to create his own product line, opening Town Tiles to create unique items for museum stores and specialty shops throughout the country.

He lives in Tampa's Hyde Park with his wife, writer Mary Scourtes Greacen, and is the father of two children, Alexandra and Scott.

Made in the USA
Monee, IL
27 March 2023

30039663R10162